MAR 1 4 2006

W9-CQS-825

...DRAWN

4.3
HUR

Agricultural Technology in the Twentieth Century

R. Douglas Hurt

ISBN 0-89745-146-5

From the April 1991 *JOURNAL of the WEST,* with an Epilogue added.

© 1991 by the
JOURNAL of the WEST, Inc.

Fort Morgan Public Library
414 Main Street
Fort Morgan, CO

Sunflower University Press®

1531 Yuma (P.O. Box 1009), Manhattan, Kansas 66502-4228, USA

Agricultural Technology in the Twentieth Century

R. Douglas Hurt

Fort Morgan Public Library
414 Main Street
Fort Morgan, CO

Wheat harvest, Wakefield, Kansas, summer 1988. (Photo by Robin Higham)

Preface

THIS study is designed for anyone who wants an introduction to the major technological changes in Western American agriculture during the twentieth century. It is a "hardware" history with a bit of social and economic analysis. My intent has been to discuss the origin and development of tractors, cotton pickers, combines, sugar beet and tomato harvesters, and irrigation technology during the twentieth century. I do not, however, discuss the political aspects of irrigation in the West or the development of the track-type tractor, which primarily serves the construction industry. Moreover, this study does not include an analysis of trucks, because the automobile, rather than agricultural technology, such as the tractor, played a primary role (along with the good roads movement during

the early twentieth century) in stimulating farmers to purchase trucks. Farmers did not begin to purchase trucks in considerable numbers until World War I increased the scarcity and cost of horses. After the war, the farm market became important for the disposal of "Liberty trucks" as manufacturers aggressively sought the rural market to maintain production of the vehicles that they had tooled to build. The adoption of the truck to agriculture merits further discussion in another forum.

In addition, I do not address the matter of financing for the technological acquisitions of farmers. This important subject merits extensive treatment, but to maintain thematic continuity, hardware remains the focus of this study. In addition, I am more concerned with the significance rather than the current operation of agricultural technology, although I have tried to bring each subject up-to-date. Space also prevented a discussion of recent developments in biotechnology. This new technological area, of course, deserves considerable historical inquiry, but that work too awaits another time and place.

Certainly, my subjects of tractors, cotton pickers, combines, sugar beet and tomato harvesters, and irrigation technology are not confined to the farming practices of the American West, but this technology is used extensively in that region. More important, this technology has made a significant contribution to the agricultural development of the United States during the twentieth century. Each technology has had far-reaching economic and social consequences. In addition, economics and society primarily influenced the development of these mechanical systems. Politics has been involved only to the extent that it affects the national economy and determines the agenda of the United States Department of Agriculture and its support of technological research at the state agricultural experiment stations.

My intent has been to synthesize and provide an overview of these major technological developments during the twentieth century. As such, this study is not designed for the specialist in agricultural history. Instead, it is directed to those who come to the subject for the first time and for agricultural history buffs who love technology. I hope, however, that both students and specialists in American agricultural history will find this work useful for review and reference.

I am grateful to a number of people who helped make this study possible. G. Terry Sharrer at the National Museum of American History in the Smithsonian Institution generously provided many photographs. Tom Root in Plymouth, Ohio, loaned several hard to find pictures of the "Silver King" tractor from his personal collection. Vicki L. Eller at the Deere & Company Archives extended crucial help. Robert Hailstock in the Photography Division of the United States Department of Agriculture, John Skarstad of the Shields Library at the University of California-Davis, Martha Vestecka-Miller at the Nebraska State Historical Society, Nancy Sherbert at the Kansas State Historical Society, Tracey Baker at the Minnesota Historical Society, and Margaret Walsh at the Colorado Historical Society helped locate photographs. Robert S. Snoozy of the Lindsay Manufacturing Company, Cindy Coffman at Valmont Industries, Van Olsen at the U.S. Sugar Beet Growers Association, and Ruthann Geib at the American Sugar Beet Growers Association provided valuable assistance with the illustrations. Laura Kline in the Special Collections of Parks Library at Iowa State University also aided this project. I completed a portion of the research for this study at the State Historical Society of Missouri and the University of Missouri-Columbia where the collections are a joy for any agricultural historian. I deeply appreciate the help that I received at those institutions. Homer E. Socolofsky and Alan I. Marcus read an early draft of this study and gave a valuable critique that enabled me to improve the manuscript. I am thankful for their time and expertise.

Portions of this work previously appeared in different form. I am grateful to the Kendall/Hunt Publishing Company for permission to excerpt from my chapter entitled "Technological Change in Twentieth-Century Agriculture," published in *Technology in the Twentieth Century*, edited by Frank J. Coppa and Richard Harmond (1983). Part of Chapter Two appeared as "P. P. Haring: Innovator in Cotton Harvesting Technology," in *Agricultural History*, 53 (Jan. 1979), and part of Chapter Five appeared as "Irrigation in the Kansas Plains Since 1930," in the *Red River Valley Historical Review*, 4 (Summer 1979). I appreciate the permission of the editors and publishers to use portions of these works.

The research for this project has been supported by a Professional Advancement Grant from Iowa State University.

Introduction

TECHNOLOGY and agriculture have been inextricably linked throughout the course of American history. During the twentieth century American agricultural technology became so innovative, practical, and affordable and so reliable and reputable that it set the standards for emulation by other countries. Indeed, with the exception of the space industry, no other area of technological development has achieved such great success and international recognition. As a result, American farmers are the most mechanized and productive agriculturists in the world, and foreign nations rely on them for food and fiber.[1]

Technological change during the twentieth century, however, did not exist in isolation. Instead, it depended upon the past. During the last half of the nineteenth century, American farmers readily adopted a host of horse-powered, labor-saving implements, such as steel swing and sulky plows, grain drills, seed planters, cultivators, self-rake reapers, binders, threshing machines, hay rakes, mowers, and feed mills. In the Great Plains and Far West, large-scale farmers also adopted steam engines for threshing and plowing.[2]

The Civil War provided the stimulus for rapid adoption of new technology, because labor shortages necessitated the adoption of machinery while high wartime prices made it affordable. With mechanization, farmers could efficiently and systematically complete more work than ever before. Mechanization helped farmers double the land in farms and boost production 135 percent between 1870 and 1900. Most of this expansion occurred in the trans-Mississippi West, where farmers purchased land from the federal government or speculators and where the semiarid climate facilitated the use of this new technology. In the Far West, for example, combines could thresh more

efficiently and operate on a greater economy of scale than in the moist, cool, Old Northwest where small-scale farms prevailed. Similarly, steam traction engines were less likely to mire on the Great Plains than in the Mississippi Delta.[3]

New implements, however, often required more power to achieve maximum efficiency than farmers could supply with their horses. Moreover, technical difficulties and economic realities kept many crops unmechanized or farmers from purchasing new equipment. The cotton crop, for example, proved particularly difficult to mechanize, while steam traction engines were too expensive and gigantic for small-scale, family farmers. Nevertheless, the technological innovations of the late nineteenth century eased the farmer's labors and expanded his economic opportunities. The development of complementing technology, such as refrigerated railway cars and canning equipment for commercial purposes, helped improve access and expand markets. Indeed, this hardware technology increased a farmer's capabilities beyond the use of animal and steam power. New machines also eliminated or greatly reduce the number of hired workers that a farmer employed at harvest time. And, this new technology made farmers more efficient and productive. As a result, they often increased their profits because of extensive production, expanded sales, and reduced labor and production costs.[4]

During the first half of the twentieth century, "hardware" dominated the technological developments in American agriculture. Technological change enabled farmers to replace animal power and human labor with mechanical power. With the wide-scale adoption of the tractor and the combine, cotton, sugar beet and tomato

The tractor was the most important form of hardware technology applied to American agriculture during the twentieth century. The International Harvester Company introduced this model F-12 in 1932. It was the smallest tractor in the Farmall series. With a four-cylinder engine, however, it had ample power to pull a grain binder. (Courtesy of the State Historical Society of Missouri)

During the twentieth century, the cotton harvester was the most important mechanical technology introduced to Southern agriculture. This two-row cotton harvester enabled one operator to handle more work than a gang of pickers. By 1984, when this photograph was taken, the cotton harvest had been mechanized for nearly 20 years. (Courtesy of the Smithsonian Institution)

harvesters, and with the adoption of sprinkler irrigation, technological change achieved revolutionary significance in American agriculture, particularly after World War II. Even so, the new technology made farmers more dependent on bankers for capital, created surplus production problems, and required agriculturists to develop better managerial skills. It also contributed to the consolidation of farms and the increase in farm size as well as to the decline in rural population. Indeed, technological change has affected millions of farmers, agricultural workers, and urbanites.[5]

After mid-twentieth century, technological change in American agriculture increasingly involved biological and chemical change, and during the last quarter of the twentieth century, biotechnology has superseded all other forms of technological research. These innovations involved the development of hybrid seeds, commercial fertilizers, herbicides, pesticides, and drugs for fighting animal diseases. Still, the hardware technology that agri-cultural engineers developed during the twentieth century has had a lasting affect on farmers and farm life.[6]

Above all, technological change is a cumulative process. Successful invention depends upon the knowledge gained from prior experience. An inventor must draw from the past — accepting, rejecting, synthesizing — to shape a new idea into a workable product. The proper use of accumulated knowledge is fundamental to innovation. Invention also depends upon perceived need and affordability. In this respect, technological change is a process rather than an event.

In contrast to the nineteenth century, however, agricultural engineers at the state experiment stations and the agricultural implement companies have achieved the major technological changes during the twentieth century. Only the agricultural experiment stations and implement companies could afford the million-dollar investment required for most technological projects. The age of the individual and independent inventor had passed. Technological change also often depended upon changing the plant to help meet the needs of the hardware as in the case of the cotton, sugar beet, and tomato harvesters. Consequently, the process of technological change became a matter of system as scientists and engineers increasingly worked in groups. They coordinated their work and readily shared the results of their research. They anticipated problems and worked within their particular area of specialization, such as plant breeding, applied entomology, or agricultural engineering, to help solve them. Between 1965 and 1980, for example, approximately 60 researchers worked at Purdue, Michigan State, and Ohio State Universities to develop a mechanical tomato harvester for growers in the Midwest. By pooling their abilities and with the large-scale funding resources available through the university and agricultural experiment station systems, these researchers could make far greater progress on technological problems than the individual inventor who worked alone at this own expense.[7]

Technology, however, is not inherently good. Invariably, it helped improve the economic and social conditions of some while it harmed the well-being of others. The tractor, for example, enabled farmers to reduce labor costs and increase efficiency. It also encouraged rapid expansion onto submarginal lands, when high agricultural prices prevailed. Many of those lands were highly erodable during periods of drought, high winds, or excessive rainfall, all to the detriment of society in general. Thus, whether technology is beneficial depends upon who owns or controls it and whether that person knows how to use it properly. Those farmers who have both the need and the money can take advantage of it, but some will benefit more than others. Certainly, technology changes a farmer's relationship to the soil and to society — sometimes for good, but other times for ill. Indeed, rapid progress and increased efficiency often have occurred at the expense of ethical, environmental, and social considerations. The cotton and tomato harvesters, for example, caused consid-

transmission sealed in an oil bath, gearing that powered both rear wheels, and pedals for brakes and clutch. In addition, the Cub had a single front wheel. Although other tractor manufacturers quickly accepted the Cub's frameless design, adoption of the narrow front end took time.

By 1915, farm implement companies were manufacturing tractors that weighed between 3,000 and 5,000 pounds and pulled two plows. Those tractors each replaced three horses in the field at plowing time and approached practicality for small-scale farmers. As a result, tractor production increased from an estimated 5 in 1900 to more than 17,000 annually. Demand for tractors also increased during World War I, when farmers in the Midwest and West increasingly used this technology to alleviate labor shortages. When the war ended, however, many farmers still could not afford a tractor or did not want one because these implements only could be used for plowing or powering stationary machinery, such as threshing machines or corn shellers. Consequently, these tractors remained unsuited for general-purpose farm work or row-crop cultivation on small-scale farms.[10]

Even so, by the beginning of World War I, the tractor industry began to mature technically with the design innovations exhibited by the Wallis Cub. Tractor engineers now knew that a farm tractor would be practical only when it could be used to complete a wide variety of farm jobs, such as pulling plows and hay wagons and powering threshing machines and fodder choppers. Tractors also had to have a good ratio of power to weight and adequate traction. Moreover, tractors had to be economical, maneuverable, and easy to maintain. In many respects, the engineers in the automobile industry had a good deal to offer their colleagues in the tractor companies.[11]

Indeed, tractor engineers quickly adopted automobile techniques, such as the use of enclosed transmissions and gear trains to replace open drive chains, roller instead of babbit bearings, and electric starters, lights, and governors. Nevertheless, most tractors remained too cumber-

In 1918, the Moline Plow Company redesigned the Universal by adding a four-cylinder engine, an electric starter, and headlights. The front drive wheels had an inner rim with concrete ballast to lower the center of gravity and reduce the tractor's tendency to pitch up. In 1924, this tractor was at work in Carroll County, Maryland. (Courtesy of the Smithsonian Institution)

In 1911, the Advance-Rumely Thresher Company built this Type E OilPull in LaPorte, Indiana. The tractor weighed 13 tons, and it had a maximum pull of 10,025 pounds. Rumely rated it with 30 drawbar and 60 belt horsepower.

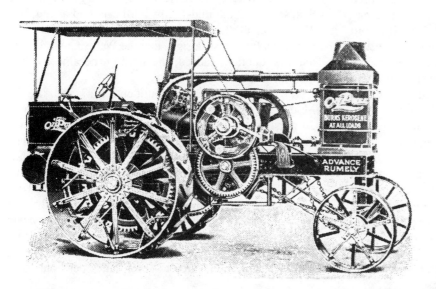

The Douch Manufacturing Company built this 15-35 model from 1912 through 1920. The four cylinders were cast separately. Known as the Sandusky Model E, it featured a rugged design and a heavy weight of 17,000 pounds.

some and expensive for the small-scale agriculturist. Farmers particularly needed a tractor that could be used for cultivation. The merger of need and design, however, took time. Until that happened, many farmers exhibited a conservative and even reactionary attitude by clinging steadfastly to their draft horses and mules in the face of great technological change.[12]

Henry Ford

While these developments occurred, Henry Ford, already establishing a reputation in automobile manufacturing, maintained that American agriculture needed to become more mechanized. No doubt Ford realized that he could easily apply his automobile assembly line to tractor production, and that a new mass market would provide a greater return on this technological investment. This is not to suggest that Ford was interested only in economic gain, because he grew up on a farm and encouraged his employees to live in the countryside. Besides being a capable inventor, Ford was a shrewd entrepreneur who deplored inefficiency. For him, horses and mules were expensive to own, because they ate too much grain and fodder. Ford believed that tractors not only provided more power than horses and mules, but also were less expensive over time as well as easier to handle. Moreover, a farmer could repair a tractor while no one could fix a dead horse with a wrench.[13]

While other inventors and entrepreneurs, then, tried to develop an efficient, affordable tractor suitable for the small-scale farmer, Ford decided to enter the field. By so doing, he left a lasting mark on the technological history of American agriculture. Between 1906 and 1908, Ford built his first tractor. It consisted of a four-cylinder, vertical engine with copper water jackets, a vibrator coil, a high-tension ignition, and a 1905 Model B Ford transmission. To these parts, he attached a radiator, hubs, steering gear, and front wheels from a Model K automobile. The rear

drive wheels came from a grain binder. Ford demonstrated this tractor on his farms near Dearborn, Michigan, where he used it to pull a binder through the wheat fields. Unfortunately, the engine did not have sufficient power to work satisfactorily, and it constantly overheated.[14]

By 1913, Ford was trying to convert a Model T chassis into a tractor by substituting a heavier frame and a stronger transmission, but this effort also failed. Two years later, however, Ford began manufacturing tractors for commercial sale. Finally, in October 1917, he produced a lightweight, low-cost, two-plow tractor called the "Fordson." All 254 tractors which he built that year went to Great Britain to aid the war effort, and he did not place his tractor on the American market until April 1918. The Fordson, however, achieved an immediate success, because of postwar shortages of men and horses for farm work, and because Ford used his automobile dealers to sell tractors. Moreover, many farmers could afford the price of $750. By 1919, nearly 34,000 Fordsons accounted for approximately 25 percent of the tractor production in the United States. During the mid-1920s, Ford captured as much as 75 percent of the tractor market, in part, because the Fordson's frameless design, like the Wallis Cub, allowed mass production. Indeed, the Fordson became the first mass-produced tractor.[15]

The original Fordson was built until 1927; and, like the Model T, it featured a simple design. The Fordson had a 20-horsepower, four-cylinder engine mounted on a cast-iron transmission housing. This design eliminated a steel frame and decreased the weight. The Fordson weighed only 2,500 pounds, and it stood less than five feet tall. The wheel base measured 63 inches, and the tractor turned in a circle of 21 feet. A low-tension magneto (attached to the flywheel) provided the spark, a thermo-siphon system cooled the engine, and an oil bath lubricated the worm gear in the rear axle. The Fordson had three forward speeds ranging from about three to seven miles per hour. Like

Waterloo Gasoline Engine Company Advertisement.

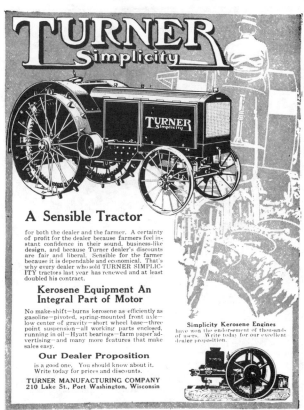

Turner Advertisement.

Wallis Cub Advertisement.

many other tractors produced at this time, it burned either kerosene or gasoline. This economy feature appealed to most farmers who thought that gasoline was too expensive. Moreover, kerosene was a readily available lamp fuel.[16]

Still, Ford's innovation had several serious problems even though it was the most practical and affordable tractor on the market. First, the Fordson was too light, and it had insufficient power to meet the needs of the farmers who tilled large acreages. Those farmers needed a tractor that could pull at least three or four plows instead of two. Moreover, the small 45-inch wheels easily mired in muddy soil, and many farmers complained the tractor was built so low to the ground that corn stalks punctured the radiator. In addition, the Fordson was difficult to start, and it had a tendency to overheat. The governor did not work properly, and it permitted great fluctuations in the engine's speed. The Fordson's most serious problem, however, was its lightness and center of gravity which caused it to rear up and flip over, whenever the drawbar encountered sudden or undue resistance. Nevertheless, the Fordson proved that small, versatile tractors could be produced at an affordable price and that such tractors could meet the power needs of many small-scale farmers. Moreover, the Fordson's design became standard, that is, conventional, for other tractor makers. With the Fordson, mass production reached the tractor industry. As a result, tractors became affordable for a large number of farmers. With the Fordson, the second revolution in American agriculture was underway.[17]

18

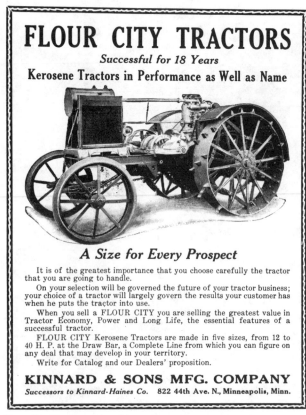

FLOUR CITY TRACTORS

Successful for 18 Years
Kerosene Tractors in Performance as Well as Name

A Size for Every Prospect

It is of the greatest importance that you choose carefully the tractor that you are going to handle.

On your selection will be governed the future of your tractor business; your choice of a tractor will largely govern the results your customer has when he puts the tractor into use.

When you sell a FLOUR CITY you are selling the greatest value in Tractor Economy, Power and Long Life, the essential features of a successful tractor.

FLOUR CITY Kerosene Tractors are made in five sizes, from 12 to 40 H. P. at the Draw Bar, a Complete Line from which you can figure on any deal that may develop in your territory.

Write for Catalog and our Dealers' proposition.

KINNARD & SONS MFG. COMPANY
Successors to Kinnard-Haines Co.   822 44th Ave. N., Minneapolis, Minn.

Flour City Tractors Advertisement.

LaCrosse Happy Farmer Tractor
The Perfect Kerosene Burner

And Only $975.00 F. O. B. Factory

And You Don't Pay Extra for Lugs and Steering Device

A TRACTOR CUSTOMER wants a tractor that will do the best possible work at the lowest possible first and upkeep costs.

A TRACTOR DEALER wants a tractor that will sell the easiest, will stay sold the longest, will help the most in selling others, and will give a good margin of profit.

Ask us direct or through any of the following for proof that the La Crosse Happy Farmer is the one that fills all the above wants.

DISTRIBUTORS

LA CROSSE TRACTOR CO. LA CROSSE WISCONSIN
Manufacturers — Not Assemblers

LaCrosse Tractor Advertisement.

Heider Tractors

Heider Tractors will be demonstrated at the National Tractor Demonstration at Salina, Kan., July 29 to Aug. 3

Model D 9-16 H. P.

The practical One Unit Plowing Outfit. A two-bottom No. 9 Rock Island Power Lift Plow attached right onto the tractor platform. Entire outfit is one unit. Foot lever control. Automatic power lift. Here is an outfit that is spelling big business for Heider dealers. Write and let us tell you more about it.

Proved by Ten Years of Actual Field Work

This proves what the Heider can do for the farmer and for the dealer who sells them.

Satisfied customers have been one of the biggest factors in the rapid growth of Heider dealers' sales.

You can always refer a prospective buyer to a Heider owner and be sure of a recommendation which helps close the sale.

The Heider Special friction transmission is one of the greatest features ever put into a farm tractor.

Seven speeds forward or reverse with one lever without disconnecting power.

Means more flexible power—less gears, less parts, less chance for breakages—lower upkeep cost.

Rock Island Branch Houses and Distributors insure prompt service to dealers and their customers.

Rock Island Plow Co.
Rock Island, Illinois

Model C 12-20 H. P.
The ideal power for the average size farm.

Heider Tractors Burn Kerosene or Gasoline

Heider Tractor Advertisement.

The 1920s

By the early 1920s, the advantages of internal-combustion tractors, compared to horses, mules, and steam traction engines, were readily apparent. Horses were expensive to purchase and costly to maintain. Farmers needed about five acres of land to supply the oats, hay, and fodder that each horse required for an entire year. In contrast, if a tractor did not work, it did not require fuel. Consequently, lands that had been used for raising animal feeds now could be seeded with more profitable cash crops for human consumption. In addition, tractors could be operated day and night, while horses and mules had to be rested or changed during the day. Compared to horses, tractors did not require as much daily care. Moreover, tractors were immune to the effects of hot weather and insects. Gasoline tractors also saved the time needed to put a steam engine into operation. Indeed, gasoline tractors started relatively easily, worked efficiently, and shut off easily. Tractors did not emit sparks from the exhaust and were safer, therefore, in the field than steam engines. Furthermore, tractors were easier to maneuver than most steam traction engines.

Still, problems remained. Only large-scale farmers with sufficient capital or credit and with land adaptable to tractors could afford to own one. Small-scale, row-crop farmers found tractors too cumbersome to maneuver in their smaller fields as well as too expensive to own. As a result, tractors remained almost entirely restricted to the western Middle West, that is, Minnesota, Iowa, and the

Great Plains, where farmers used them for plowing and powering threshing machines. In this respect, gasoline tractors remained about as useful and practical as steam traction engines. Moreover, row crops, such as corn and cotton, require cultivation, and tractors, such as the Fordson, could not be driven down the rows without damaging the plants. Indeed, tractors could perform only about 38 percent of the necessary work involved with raising row crops. Consequently, most farmers delayed the purchase of a tractor until an all-purpose implement could pull both plows and cultivators, and until it could be purchased for a reasonable price.[18]

The Farmall

In 1924, the International Harvester Company contributed to the great technological change underway in American agriculture by introducing the Farmall tractor which soon made the Fordson obsolete. The Farmall was the first low-priced, tricycle-designed tractor built for row-crop farming. In front, the Farmall had two closely spaced wheels designed to travel between the crop rows. In the rear, it had a high axle to straddle the growing crop, and a brake on each rear wheel enabled quick, sharp turns. It had three forward speeds and a reverse. Although the Fordson was too light for tractor work on grain farms, it was ideal for truck and dairy farms. And, by 1925, small tractors, such as the Farmall, were in wide use on dairy, vegetable, and fruit farms from New York to the Pacific Coast. A decade later virtually all tractor manufacturers built one or more models of an all-purpose tractor and, in 1937, three-fourths of all tractors sold in the United States were general-purpose tractors.[19]

The Farmall, introduced by the International Harvester Company in 1924, was the first practical and affordable row-crop tractor. It featured brake control on the steering column, the ability to pivot on either rear wheel, and a turning radius of eight feet. (Courtesy of the Smithsonian Institution)

In 1924, Deere & Company built the first Model D. This tractor remained in production until 1953. Its two-cylinder engine provided reliability and economy. Farmers liked the Model D because, it was both rugged and simple to repair. (Courtesy of the Smithsonian Institution)

In 1947, the Farmall Cub was the smallest tractor built by IHC. It could pull one plow, and it served anyone who needed modest tractor power. IHC discontinued the Cub in 1964. (Courtesy of the Smithsonian Institution)

IHC also equipped the Farmall with a power takeoff (PTO) which it had introduced perhaps as early as 1918. The power takeoff enabled the tractor to drive the mechanisms of the implements which it pulled, such as spraying, dusting, and fertilizing equipment. The PTO transferred the power from the tractor's engine directly to the implement in use, via a splined drive shaft at the rear of the tractor. A clutch engaged the PTO gearing that linked the tractor and the implement. By so doing, the PTO replaced the cumbersome bull wheel which drove the machine's mechanisms when set into operation by draft power. It also replaced gasoline engines that farmers attached to their implements to power the working parts.

The PTO helped make tractors suitable for small-scale farmers. The Farmall could cultivate four rows at once, or pull a binder, corn picker, or mower. The Farmall probably did more to prove the value and versatility of the tractor and to stimulate further farm mechanization than any other implement. Indeed, the PTO improved the tractor's utility, further reduced human labor, and made the completion of farm tasks, such as harvesting and mowing, easier and more efficient than ever before. The PTO also eventually ended the production of tractors with beltwork capabilities, that is, for powering threshing machines and fodder choppers.[20]

Other innovations soon followed as tractor engineers and manufacturers developed various oil, water bath, and paper filters to keep the dust out of the tractor's engine and prolong its life. Engineers also improved the power-to-weight ratios which helped stabilize and increase drawbar power. Some engineers experimented with generators, batteries, and electrical systems to replace the hard and often aggravating job of cranking the tractor by hand with a self-starting system.[21]

Improvements

Three major refinements, however, substantially improved the operating efficiency of the tractor. First, in 1928, John Deere added a power lift to enable the driver to raise plows, discs, and cultivators from the soil without leaving the tractor. This innovation enabled easier turning at the end of the crop row, and it made the tractor more maneuverable in small fields. Power lifts also eased a farmer's labors by eliminating the drudgery and hard work of getting up and down from the tractor to raise or lower an implement at the beginning or end of each row in order to make a turn. Second, in 1932, Allis-Chalmers added pneumatic tires to the tractor in place of iron or steel rims. This innovation produced a more comfortable ride, reduced wear on tractor parts, permitted faster speeds, and decreased fuel costs from 10 to 20 percent. Rubber tires also meant that tractors could be used for pulling wagons and other implements without damaging road surfaces with lugged, iron wheels. Tractors used in this manner

In 1928, Massey-Harris Company produced the 26-41 model Wallis, known as Model 25. Tractors with power take-off enabled farmers to provide consistent and adequate power for implements such as this corn picker. The power takeoff system meant that implements no longer needed a separate engine to drive the mechanisms or to depend on a ground wheel for power. (Courtesy of the Parks Library, Iowa State University)

The Avery Company of Peoria, Illinois, introduced this six-cylinder, two-row motor cultivator in 1919. The driver operated the tractor from the rear, much like driving a team of horses. (Courtesy of the Parks Library, Iowa State University)

This Farmall, with a power takeoff system, enabled a farmer to power a grain binder and other equipment. During the 1940s, the binder, threshing machine, and tractor became one implement in the form of the self-propelled combine. (Courtesy of the Parks Library, Iowa State University)

Although a tractor gave farmers greater power, it also required adjustment of old equipment or the purchase of new implements because horse-drawn implements usually proved unsuitable. The adaptation of the complimentary technology took time. Here, a farmer uses a cumbersome cultivator that he has attached to the front of his tractor. (Courtesy of the Parks Library, Iowa State University)

The J. I. Case Threshing Machine Company introduced their Model CC during the early 1930s. It marked the entry of Case into the row-crop implement field. Here, the tractor powers a hay baler. (Courtesy of the Parks Library, Iowa State University)

During the 1920s, the Hart-Parr 16-30 was one of the company's popular lightweight tractors. It featured the injection of water into the cylinder to prevent premature ignition or "pinging." Here, the tractor powers a baler. (Courtesy of the Parks Library, Iowa State University)

freed the farm truck for other work and helped eliminate draft horses from the farm. Farmers quickly recognized and appreciated these benefits and by 1940, 90 percent of all new tractors sold had pneumatic tires. Third, in 1939, Henry Ford became the first American tractor manufacturer to use the "three-point hitch" of Harry Ferguson, a Belfast inventor. This hitch used a hydraulic system to keep a plow or cultivator automatically at a preset depth, regulated the downward thrust on the rear wheels when the draft power increased, and enabled more efficient use of the engine's power. By the following year, tractor gearing also had been improved to increase road speeds up to 20 miles per hour and to permit field speeds of three to five miles per hour. Faster speeds, however, required the redesign of many implements originally made for horse power.[22]

Tractor Testing

Not all tractor companies, however, were interested in improving their implements. During the 1920s, many fly-by-night companies defrauded the farmers with watered stock, empty promises, and poorly made tractors. With 100 companies manufacturing tractors by 1920, the quality of the implements varied considerably. Many of the disreputable companies acquired surplus engines from various makers, bought wheels from a local blacksmith, placed the engine on a frame, and linked engine and wheels with a transmission, often in a haphazard manner. Frequently, the tractor salesmen from these firms were little different from the seed and nursery salesmen who plagued farmers during the late nineteenth century with their "oily" tongues and shoddy products. Usually, the results were the same. By the time the farmer realized that he had purchased a faulty product, the salesman and his company were long gone. Moreover, the farmer was fortunate if he could obtain spare parts for his nearly unique tractor. Indeed, prior to the mass production of the Fordson, standardized parts for tractors did not exist. All parts had to be fitted by hand. Soon, farmers requested consumer protection from some authoritative governmental agency, such as the United States Department of Agriculture. Specifically, farmers wanted a system of uniform testing to enable them to know precisely the capabilities of any model by any company.[23]

In 1919, tractor manufacturers, farmers, and representatives from the agricultural colleges and trade organizations called for national testing by a new Bureau of Agricultural Engineering in the United States Department of Agriculture. These calls fell on deaf ears in Congress. In that same year, however, the Nebraska legislature, which included farmers who had had bad experiences with poorly made tractors, approved a bill that required all companies that sold tractors in Nebraska to submit their implements for official testing. The tractor tests were to be supervised by a three-man board of engineers at the University of Nebraska. In mid-July 1919, the University of Nebraska began tractor testing. Although federal legislation and testing was not forthcoming, the Nebraska tests soon set the national and international standards for measuring tractor performance and became an early result of consumer legislation designed to protect farmers.[24]

The officials who conducted the tractor tests sought out defective valves, blocks and heads, and other inferior parts. They also tested for performance, checked fuel consumption, measured slippage, and compared the test results to the advertising of the tractor companies. If the results did not compare accurately with the claims, the tractor companies had to change their advertising or improve their implements; only then could their tractors be sold in Nebraska. In time, the Nebraska tests became the equivalent of the "Good House Keeping Seal of Approval," as well as an official consumer report, which not only protected farmers but also helped the companies sell more

tractors, if their implements met or exceeded the Nebraska requirements. With the help of the American Society of Agricultural Engineers and the Society of Automobile Engineers, implement manufacturers also made additional improvements, such as standardizing the drawbar height for hitches and PTO sizes, speeds, and rotational direction. These design changes further improved tractor performance and versatility and helped the tractor manufacturers standardize other agricultural equipment.[25]

These technological improvements, whether forced or voluntary, helped convince farmers that tractors could provide cheap, dependable power. Although only 3.6 percent of the American farmers owned tractors in 1920, by 1930, 13.5 percent had adopted the implement for their farm operations. A decade later, 23 percent owned tractors and more farmers probably would have made the necessary investment had not low agricultural prices, drought, and overproduction brought economic hardships to many farm families throughout the 1920s and 1930s. Indeed, economic hard times discouraged most farmers from purchasing tractors. During the Great Depression of the 1930s, for example, declining farm prices and low labor costs, together with the farmer's ability to produce feed crops, made horses cheaper to own than tractors.[26]

General Adoption

Despite these problems, by 1940, the corn and cash grain farmers in the Midwest and Great Plains had the highest percentage of tractors. Those regions were well suited for complete mechanization because tractors easily could pull plows, drills, and combines or corn pickers over the relatively level terrain and larger fields. Southern farmers, however, were slower to adopt tractors because other technological problems prevented the complete

By the late 1920s, this wide-tread, general-purpose tractor enabled farmers to cultivate two or plant three rows at one time. (Courtesy of the Deere & Company Archives)

In 1928, Deere & Company introduced the "GP" or general-purpose tractor. The tractor remained in production until 1935. In addition to draft, it also provided belt power for a host of farm implements, such as this feed grinder. (Courtesy of the Deere & Company Archives)

In 1933, the Fate-Root-Heath Company in Plymouth, Ohio, began producing tractors. The "Plymouth" had a four-cylinder engine, weighed 2,170 pounds, and reached a road speed of 25 miles per hour. This 10-20 model was designed for the small-scale farmer, who only needed to pull one or two plows. (Courtesy of Tom Root)

mechanization of staple crops, such as cotton, tobacco, and rice.

Nevertheless, where farmers adopted the tractor, this implement enabled swift completion of tillage, planting, and harvesting operations. Plowing, for example, requires the greatest amount of power of any farm operation. At the turn of the twentieth century, a farmer could plow one acre in 1.8 hours. By 1938, a tractor enabled him to till that same area in 30 minutes. By 1970, farmers could plow one acre every four minutes with a tractor, and farmers em-

ployed five million of these implements for a ratio of more than one per farm. The tractor not only gave farmers the ability to till their land faster, but it also enabled them to cultivate more acres. Since each tractor generated far more power than a horse, a farmer could use larger machinery to cover more ground without maintaining a large herd of horses or mules. As a result, tractors, together with other large and improved field implements, helped reduce crop production unit costs and thereby gave the farmer more profit for his labors.[27]

During World War II, high prices and labor shortages encouraged farmers to purchase more tractors. Between 1941 and 1945, the price of corn and wheat, for example, increased from 75 cents to $1.23 per bushel and from 94 cents to $1.49 per bushel, respectively. Farmers recognized that expanded production would enable them to reap large profits from high wartime prices and that tractors provided the means to expand productivity far more rapidly than horses or mules. With the aid of tractors, farmers increased corn and wheat production by more than nine million and two million acres, respectively, during the war years. Frequently, the farm wife drove the tractor, because it was easier to handle than a team of horses. By the end of the war 30.5 percent of the farmers in the United States used tractors. Put another way, nearly 690,000 new tractors had displaced two million horses and mules between 1941 and 1945. Tractors now were adaptable to nearly every American farm. As farmers increasingly replaced horses and mules with tractors, they gained additional land for cash crops. By 1950 more than three million tractors had freed an estimated 70 million acres for the production of food and fiber. As more farmers adopted the tractor the number of horses and mules on American farms continued to decline; and, in 1955, tractors exceeded the number of farm horses for the first time. Not long thereafter the Statistical Reporting Service for the United States Depart-

In 1935, the Plymouth tractor was renamed the "Silver King" because of a prior automotive claim by the Chrysler Corporation. This tricycle model appeared in 1936. With a road speed of 30 miles per hour, it probably was the fastest tractor during the 1940s. (Courtesy of Tom Root)

This John Deere 4320 diesel-powered tractor harvested a corn crop for fodder near Vandalia, Missouri, in 1974. The weights on the front of the tractor helped balance the force exerted by the forage harvester and wagon on the rear tires. (Courtesy of the University of Missouri Agricultural Extension)

ment of Agriculture stopped counting the number of farm horses and mules; and, by the 1980s, the draft horse was little more than a novelty on the American farm.[28]

Conclusion

In retrospect, as early as 1910, many large-scale farmers believed that tractors would save time and effort and by so doing increase production and leisure. Tractors enabled farmers to plant and harvest more acres than ever before, cotton being the major exception. These implements also required less time to start than steam engines and fewer hours at the end of the day than a team of horses that had to be fed and watered. With a flick of a switch, a tractor could be shut off and left in the field until the next day. Or, it could be unhitched from plow, cultivator, or mower and driven home and parked in the farmyard. Tractors also

eventually became status symbols for most farmers. Many farmers no doubt bought a tractor, even those who really did not need one or who could not afford the implement, because to neighbors and residents in town it symbolized progressive farming with the most advanced technology.[29]

Although tractors increased the acreage that farmers could plant and decreased the drudgery of riding a sulky plow behind a team of horses or mules as well as brought increased prestige to the farmers who owned them, this technology also created new problems for farmers. Tractors, for example, made agriculturists vulnerable to world politics that inflated the price of oil and fuel. The first problem, of course, was more immediate than the latter which did not emerge as a major factor for determining the cost of farming until the late twentieth century. Tractors also required farmers to become skillful mechanics.[30]

Although tractors saved time for farmers, increased

This International Harvester tractor featured an all-weather cab, heater, and air conditioner. In addition, to these conveniences, the power takeoff enabled compatibility with the new farm implements built during the 1970s, such as this hay press. (Courtesy of the University of Missouri Agricultural Extension, photo by Duane Dailey)

After World War II, tractor manufacturers began building larger tractors in contrast to previous efforts to reduce size and weight. By 1960, few manufacturers produced tractors of less than 50-horsepower. In 1971, this four-wheel drive John Deere Model 7520 pulled six drills. (Courtesy of the Deere & Company Archives)

leisure did not mean that a farmer spent that extra time sitting on the front porch. Rather, more free time enabled farmers to tackle other tasks which they ordinarily would have delayed or which they would have hired workers to complete. Farmers also had to use the time saved by the tractor to earn additional money to meet the payments on the implement or to defray the mortgage on the new lands that they had purchased for the purpose of expanding their operations with the help of this new technology. Thus, while the tractor saved the farmer time and effort and increased his efficiency, it also made him work harder for a longer time. It was the carrot of self-efficiency![31]

In 1924, the McCormick-Deering branch of the International Harvester Company introduced the Farmall tractor. The tricycle design of this tractor enabled farmers to cultivate between the crop rows. The Farmall had individually operated rear wheel brakes that permitted the driver to pivot the implement on either wheel for short, sharp turns in small fields. The Farmall was well suited for a host of agricultural jobs, including pushing sweep rakes for gathering the hay crop. (From *The Rise of the Wheat State: A History of Kansas Agriculture, 1861-1986*, by George E. Ham and Robin Higham, eds.)

The introduction of the Farmall tricycle tractor in 1924 proved to be the event that doomed the use of horses and mules for row crop production. It was highly maneuverable and could work long hours in hot weather. (From *The Rise of the Wheat State: A History of Kansas Agriculture, 1861-1986*, by George E. Ham and Robin Higham, eds.)

While the tractor became the key to the mechanization of the farm, it also helped cause the industrialization of agriculture and the technological revolution that has led to modern agribusiness industry. Moreover, the tractor helped end farming as a way of life. When a farmer purchased a tractor and equipment specially designed to meet the draft capabilities of this new implement, he often borrowed from the bank to finance this technology. In order to be received favorably by loan officers, farmers had to prove they were good managers of their capital and land. Large

loans mandated that farmers keep better financial records, increase production, and decrease unit costs. With the adoption of the tractor, the pace of farm life began to quicken.[32]

The diversified farms that fed families and communities required more specialized equipment and greater capital investment than did specialized, one-crop agriculture. Consequently, farmers who bought tractors increasingly concentrated on the production of one or two crops, such as wheat, corn, or sorghum grains. These crops produced the greatest volume and thereby reduced unit costs and provided the highest returns on their investment. While farmers increased the production of these crops, they also drastically reduced their acreages of forage crops, because they had less need for horses and mules. Increased acreage devoted to commercial crops, together with higher yields due to better timing for planting, cultivating, and harvesting with the aid of a tractor, however, frequently caused overproduction and low prices. Farmers then tried to offset low prices by planting more acres.[33]

Tractors also decreased the need for hired labor, tenants, and sharecroppers for most aspects of crop production except cotton. While economists calculate the tractor's savings in man-hours and money to the farmer, these implements had a more personal influence on people than the sterile statistics indicate. Indeed, the savings of time and money meant that many farm workers left the land to seek jobs elsewhere. Whether they improved their condition, no one can accurately say. Some, no doubt, improved their fortunes, while others probably regretted that technological change had altered the course of their lives forever.[34]

The tractor also had other affects on American agriculture. By enabling farmers to plant and harvest more acres, small-scale farmers often could not compete, particularly when surplus production drove prices down. As a result, farm sizes continued to increase as the small-scale farmers sold out and withdrew from agriculture. Moreover, tractors decreased the need for large families to help with the farm work. Smaller families, larger farms, and fewer agricultural workers and farmers have had a corresponding influence on the small towns in the countryside. These changes, together with new forms of transportation, such as cars and trucks, have changed marketing and purchasing patterns in rural America. Although the tractor is not responsible entirely for the demise of small towns, this technology helped eliminate many people from the countryside. Fewer people meant that local merchants often could not earn sufficient profits to remain in business. Tractors also compact the soil, and this retards drainage and root penetration. Tractors, however, enabled those who remained on the farm to extend their working lives longer than ever before. When a farmer began to lose the strength and spring in his legs, his livelihood was not in jeopardy, because he still could use the tractor to help complete his farm tasks relatively easily. All of these results did not happen overnight, but these effects became increasingly apparent and important following the rapid adoption of tractors during the World War II.[35]

Without a doubt, the tractor has been the vanguard of technological change in American agriculture. Tractors, for example, required agricultural engineers to redesign the plows, cultivators, and mowing machines that farmers used with horse-drawn implements, because that equipment was unsuitable for the stress and wear caused by the tractor's power, and because it did not work as efficiently as specially designed equipment. By the early 1980s, 1.9 million farms used 4.5 million tractors for an average of nearly 2.4 tractors per farm. Many of those tractors had sufficient power to pull multiple-hitch rigs, including plows, grain drills, and liquid fertilizer, pesticide and herbicide applicators.

Today, the tractor has not solved all farm problems. In fact, this implement has created new ones which still trouble life in rural America. Nor have tractors been able to supply all power requirements on the farm. Trucks, for example, provide a cheaper and more convenient and efficient way to haul grain and livestock to market than do tractors and wagons. Instead, tractors primarily are used for pulling implements through or over the soil, just as in the past. With the exception of improvements, such as cabs, air conditioning, and stereos, the basic structure of the tractor has not changed substantially since the early 1920s. Nevertheless, the tractor has become such an important agricultural implement that only special groups, such as the Old Order Amish, can claim to be farmers without one.[36]

NOTES

1. R. Douglas Hurt, *American Farm Tools: From Hand-Power to Steam-Power* (Manhattan, KS: Sunflower University Press, 1982).
2. R. B. Gray, *The Agricultural Tractor, 1855-1950*, pt. 1 (St. Joseph, MI: American Society of Agricultural Engineers, 1975), 14-15; John T. Schlebecker, *Whereby We Thrive: A History of American Farming, 1607-1972* (Ames: Iowa State University Press, 1975), 202.
3. Schlebecker, *Whereby We Thrive*, 202; C. H. Wendel, *Encyclopedia of American Farm Tractors* (Sarasota, FL: Crestline Publishing Co., 1975), 72.
4. Schlebecker, *Whereby We Thrive*, 202.
5. Gray, *The Agricultural Tractor*, pt. 1: 18, 23; Philip S. Rose, "Farm Tractors: A Review of Their History, Condition of Use and Methods of Construction," *Scientific American Supplement*, 81 (29 Apr. 1916): 282. Robert C. Williams, *Fordson, Farmall, and Poppin' Johnny: A History of the Farm Tractor and Its Impact on America* (Urbana: University of Illinois Press, 1987), 17. Actually, the word "tractor" was first used in an 1890 patent.
6. Gray, *The Agricultural Tractor*, pt. 1: 28; Reynold M. Wik, "Henry Ford's Tractors and American Agriculture," *Agricultural History*, 38 (Apr. 1964): 81.
7. Rose, "Farm Tractors," 282; Schlebecker, *Whereby We Thrive*, 204; Williams, *Fordson, Farmall, and Poppin' Johnny*, 18-19; Alan I Marcus and Howard P. Segal, *Technology in America, A Brief History* (San Diego: Harcourt Brace Jovanovich, Publishers, 1989), 276.
8. Marcus and Segal, *Technology in America*, 276; Williams, *Fordson, Farmall, and Poppin' Johnny*, 19-20.
9. Williams, *Fordson, Farmall, and Poppin' Johnny*, 23-24.
10. E. J. Baker, "A Quarter Century of Tractor Development," *Agricultural Engineering*, 12 (June 1931): 206; Williams, *Fordson, Farmall, and Poppin' Johnny*, 25.
11. Wiiliams, *Fordson, Farmall, and Poppin' Johnny*, 27, 35.
12. *Ibid.*, 27-28, 31, 33-34.
13. Wik, "Henry Ford's Tractors," 79; Reynold M. Wik, "Henry Ford's Science and Technology for Rural America," *Technology and Culture*, 3 (Summer 1962): 248.
14. Wik, "Henry Ford's Tractors," 80, 83; Wendel, *Encyclopedia of American Farm Tractors*, 113; Marcus and Segal, *Technology in America*, 270-272.
15. John T. Schlebecker, "Henry Ford's Tractor," *Smithsonian Journal of History*, 2 (Summer 1967): 63; Hiram M. Drache, *Beyond the Furrow: Some Keys to Successful Farming in the Twentieth Century* (Danville, IL: Interstate Printers, 1976), 30; Williams, *Fordson, Farmall, and Poppin' Johnny*, 55.
16. Wik, "Henry Ford's Tractors," 84. Williams, *Fordson, Farmall, and Poppin' Johnny*, 48. In 1931, the Caterpillar Tractor Company of Peoria, Illinois, built the first diesel-powered tractor in the United States.
17. Wik, "Henry Ford's Tractors," 83-84, 86; Williams, *Fordson, Farmall, and Poppin' Johnny*, 49, 54.
18. Williams, *Fordson, Farmall, and Poppin' Johnny*, 71-72, 76-77; D. C. Heitshu, "The Requirements of the General-Purpose Farm Tractor," *Agricultural Engineering*, 10 (May 1929): 155.
19. Gray, *The Agricultural Tractor*, pt. 2: 9; Drache, *Beyond the Furrow*, 31; Williams, *Fordson, Farmall, and Poppin' Johnny*, 90.
20. Williams, *Fordson, Farmall, and Poppin' Johnny*, 62-64; Marcus and Segal, *Technology in America*, 277; Heitshu, "The Requirements of the General-Purpose Farm Tractor," 155. In 1906 Albert Gougis developed the PTO in France. Ed Johnson, an IHC employee who had worked for Gougis, brought the PTO design to the United States, but the date is uncertain. In 1922 the McCormick-Deering Company marketed the 15-30 model tractor with a power takeoff. This tractor probably was the first implement designed specifically with a PTO system.
21. Williams, *Fordson, Farmall, and Poppin' Johnny*, 64-65.
22. Schlebecker, *Whereby We Thrive*, 248-249; Gray, *The Agricultural Tractor*, pt. 2: 15-16; Colin Fraser, *Tractor Pioneer: The Life of Harry Ferguson* (Athens: Ohio University Press, 1973), 67-73, 109-119; Williams, *Fordson, Farmall, and Poppin' Johnny*, 91, 93, 103.
23. Louis I. Leviticus, "Tractor Testing in the World," *Agricultural History*, 54 (Jan. 1980); 167; Williams, *Fordson, Farmall, and Poppin' Johnny*, 66-67.
24. Leviticus, "Tractor Testing in the World," 167; Williams, *Fordson, Farmall, and Poppin' Johnny*, 67-69; Robert E. Stewart, *Seven Decades That Changed America: A History of the American Society of Agricultural Engineers, 1907-1977* (St. Joseph, MI: American Society of Agricultural Engineers, 1979), 75.
25. Leviticus, "Tractor Testing in the World," 168; Williams, *Fordson, Farmall, and Poppin' Johnny*, 70; Marcus and Segal, *Technology in America*, 277.
26. Gilbert C. Fite, *American Farmers: The New Minority* (Bloom-

ington: Indiana University Press, 1981), 70; Robert E. Ankli and Alan L. Olmstead, "The Adoption of the Gasoline Tractor in California," *Agricultural History*, 55 (July 1981): 213, 217; Robert E. Ankli, "Horses vs. Tractors on the Corn Belt," *Agricultural History*, 54 (Jan. 1980): 139-147.

27. Fite, *American Farmers*, 70-71; Richard S. Kirkendall, "Up to Now: A History of American Agriculture From Jefferson to Revolution to Crisis," *Agriculture and Human Values*, 4 (Winter 1987): 11.

28. *Historical Statistics of the United States: Colonial Times to 1970*, pt. 1 (Washington, D.C.: Government Printing Office, 1975), 511, 517, 519; Drache, *Beyond the Furrow*, 48; Williams, *Fordson, Farmall, and Poppin' Johnny*, 96; Pete Daniel, *Breaking the Land: The Transformation of Cotton, Tobacco, and Rice Cultures Since 1880* (Urbana: University of Illinois Press, 1985), 333.

29. Fite, *American Farmers*, 184; Williams, *Fordson, Farmall, and Poppin' Johnny*, 131-133.

30. Williams, *Fordson, Farmall, and Poppin' Johnny*, 133.

31. *Ibid.*, 134.

32. *Ibid.*, 137; John L. Shover, *First Majority — Last Minority: The Transformation of Rural Life in America* (Dekalb: Northern Illinois University Press, 1976), 149.

33. Williams, *Fordson, Farmall, and Poppin' Johnny*, 138, 149; Schlebecker, *Whereby We Thrive*, 205.

34. Daniel, *Breaking the Land*, 176, 183; Williams, *Fordson, Farmall, and Poppin' Johnny*, 157.

35. Williams, *Fordson, Farmall, and Poppin' Johnny*, 155, 178-179.

36. .Gilbert C. Fite, *Cotton Fields No More: Southern Agriculture, 1865-1980* (Lexington: University of Kentucky Press), 102; *1982 Census of Agriculture*, I: 9; Sam B. Hilliard, " The Dynamics of Power: Recent Trends in Mechanization on the American Farm," *Technology and Culture*, 13 (Jan. 1972): 14-15; Williams, *Fordson, Farmall, and Poppin' Johnny*," 74, 123-124.

Chapter 2

Cotton Pickers and Strippers

WHILE some agricultural engineers and entrepreneurs, such as Henry Ford, worked to develop a reliable internal-combustion tractor, others devoted their attention to the most important regional problem in twentieth-century agricultural technology — mechanizing the cotton harvest. Through the first half of the twentieth century, however, the cotton harvest differed little from antiquity. Indeed, technological change came slowly to this aspect of American agriculture, and nearly a century would pass from the patent of the first cotton picker in 1850 until the International Harvester Company (IHC) began quantity production of a mechanical picker in 1948.

In order to develop a cotton picker, agricultural engi-

neers faced a multiplicity of problems — diverse soil and climatic conditions, various plant types and ripening times, technical and economic difficulties, and an abundance of cheap farm labor. Above all, a marketable cotton picker had to be reasonably priced and easy to operate and repair; it had to be maneuverable on moderately rough terrain and in muddy fields; and, it had to pick a high percentage of trash-free cotton without damaging the lint.[1]

Early Developments

The solutions to these problems were not easy. In fact, inventors patented more than 1,800 cotton pickers be-

Until the 1950s, workers harvested most of the cotton crop by hand. Although inventors had tried to build a mechanical harvester for more than a century by that time, the nature of the cotton plant slowed mechanization, because the crop did not ripen uniformly. Workers customarily picked a field three times. When scientists changed the plant to meet once-over harvesting requirements, agricultural engineers could perfect a mechanical harvester. (Courtesy of the Charles Trefts Photography Collection, State Historical Society of Missouri)

Pneumatic machines were among the earliest mechanical harvesters. Essentially, these implements were giant vacuum cleaners designed to suck the fiber from the bolls. The operator held the hose to a boll and the fiber passed to a detachable bag in the rear of the machine. This pneumatic picker was mounted on a Beeman garden tractor. The engine powered the vacuum for these demonstrators in December 1919, near Little Rock, Arkansas. (Courtesy of the Smithsonian Institution)

In 1891 Peter Paul Haring of Goliad, Texas, began experimenting with a spindle picker. This model, probably built about 1929, shows the prong spindles designed to lift the fiber from the bolls. As the picker moved forward, the wheels powered the machine. Haring could not perfect this machine, and the Great Depression ended his efforts. (Courtesy of the Smithsonian Institution)

tween 1850 and 1942, when the International Harvester Company tested the first reliable implement. These numerous inventions included: threshing machines that cut the entire plant and separated the cotton from the bolls in a process similar to a grain combine; pneumatic pickers that removed the cotton from the bolls with suction or blasts of air; electrical machines that used static electricity to extract the cotton; strippers that pulled the entire boll from the stalk; and spindles that used fingers and prongs to remove the lint.[2]

The pneumatic machines operated much like giant vacuum cleaners. When the operator touched the end of the hose to a boll, it sucked the lint into a tank or bag. In 1918 a pneumatic machine harvested a small portion of the cotton crop in California's Imperial Valley. Four years later, the IHC began experiments with a pneumatic picker and tested both suction and air-blast models during the next few years. In 1924 one of these experimental models consisted of a large diaphragm vacuum pump driven by an eight-horsepower gasoline engine. This pneumatic picker was mounted on a two-wheel cart pulled by a mule. Four hoses enabled the operators to suck the cotton into a large bag at the end of the cart. This machine, however, harvested less cotton than one hand picker in the same amount of time, and hand-picked cotton had less trash in the fiber. In 1925 IHC also tested a cotton-threshing machine modeled after a grain separator. This implement pulled the boll

In 1927, Deere & Company tested a cotton stripper near Plainview, Texas. Two years later the company built this two-row, tractor-mounted stripper. As the plant entered the machine, metal teeth stripped the fiber from the boll and passed it to an elevator which deposited the cotton in a container attached behind the tractor. (Courtesy of the Deere & Company Archives)

off the plant and separated the lint from the thrash. The cotton thresher, however, proved defective because the machine harvested immature as well as ripe bolls. It also failed to separate effectively, and it clogged easily.[3]

In 1922 T. C. Stuckenborg, a Memphis inventor, attempted to use both electricity and a vacuum machine to extract the lint from cotton bolls. He built a machine with electrically powered brushes that revolved inward. Mounted on a gasoline tractor, the engine powered eight electric motors, which drove eight picking brushes and eight cleaning fans. This machine also failed to outperform hand pickers. Indeed, the rate of failure was high among the inventors who tried to mechanize the cotton harvest. Of all these various harvesters, only the strippers and spindle pickers proved successful. The other implements were overly complicated, technically imperfect, or still required some form of hand labor to operate properly.[4]

Progress in cotton harvesting technology lagged until the late nineteenth century when several men began experimenting with rotating spindles for extracting the fiber from the bolls. In 1885 Angus Campbell, an engineer at the Deering Harvester Company in Chicago, started work on a spindle picker that used a series of rotating fingers to twist and pull the fiber from the bolls. Campbell field-tested his machine in 1889, but he did not patent it

until 1895. For the next 20 years at picking time, Campbell transported his models to the South. During that time, he tested 55 spindle pickers, but inadequate shop facilities and the relatively short picking season hindered perfection of his design. In 1910, Campbell joined Theodore H. Price who also had patented a spindle picker. The Price-Campbell cotton picker, patented in 1912, resulted from this partnership. Both men made additional improvements on their harvester for the next ten years. The machine, however, never reached perfection, because it was too complicated and too expensive to build. Moreover, it did not pick enough cotton from the bolls; it broke down the plants as it traveled through the fields; and it damaged the unopened bolls which decreased the harvest from the second picking.[5]

Other inventors, such as Peter Paul Haring of Goliad, Texas, also experimented with spindle pickers without success. In many respects, Haring typifies the private, independent inventors who attempted to build a mechanical cotton harvester and who failed. In 1891, Haring's first machine did not pick much cotton, and he did not patent it. Haring evidently experimented with a series of spindle picking fingers not unlike those used on his later patented models. In 1897 he patented a cotton picker that featured revolving drums with radial tubular arms carrying flared rotating picker points or fingers. The four-wheeled frame could carry one or more pairs of drums. Haring arranged each pair of drums so that a row of cotton passed between them. A sprocket chain attached to the rear axle caused the drums to rotate inward. As the drums revolved, the picking points also turned, caught the cotton, and twisted it from the boll. After the arms carried the cotton to the outside of the machine, the picking points reversed rotation, thus disengaging the fiber and dropping it onto a conveyor. The cotton then passed into a container at the front of the machine.[6]

Haring turned this cotton picker over to the McCormick Harvesting Machine Company for tests, but the company was not impressed with the results. After running the machine down one row four or five times, the technicians could not distinguish whether any cotton had been picked. The picking arms merely brushed the bolls away, broke them off, or failed to reach them, and the picking points dropped the cotton that was picked to the ground. McCormick tested the machine for several days and acknowledged: "For a first machine it was well built and as perfect as it would be possible to make it were we again to rebuild

In 1942, IHC field-tested its first commercially viable mechanical harvester in the Mississippi Delta. By the end of the decade, farmers used nearly 1,500 cotton pickers to harvest the crop. (Courtesy of the Smithsonian Institution)

As early as 1902, the agricultural engineers at IHC began planning for a mechanical harvester. After 40 years of work and an expenditure of $5.2 million, it built the first successful spindle picker. In 1945, this machine harvested in the South. (Courtesy of the Smithsonian Institution)

it." Nevertheless, the company decided the cotton picker was not a "promise of success" and gave up further experimentation with it.[7]

Haring, like other inventors, was not discouraged with the results of the McCormick tests and persisted in his attempts to develop an efficient cotton picker. In 1905, Haring patented an improved design in which he replaced the drums with slats that traveled in elliptical guides attached to the frame. He designed the picking fingers to engage the cotton more readily, hold it, and free the fiber at the proper time. Haring also increased the number of picking points and extended them from all sides of the arms or spindles. On his original machine, he had only attached the picking points to the top and bottom of the spindles. He bent the picking fingers in a corkscrew fashion to enable them to grasp the cotton more firmly and to release the fiber upon reversing their rotation.[8]

After making additional improvements on the cotton picker, Haring organized the Haring Cotton Machine Company in 1910. Theoretically, the company's purpose was to manufacture and sell farm machinery. In reality, however, the company provided Haring with the time and financial support to continue refining his cotton harvester. He patented a machine much like the 1905 model the following year. Haring, however, had increased the capacity of the harvester and changed the release mechanism to improve the disengagement of the cotton from the picking fingers. He constantly sought to improve his latest model, and in 1913 patented another design. By that time Haring had changed the picking fingers to consist of two hook-shaped points which, operating on his previously patented principle, twisted firmly into the cotton. He also simplified the machine's structure with the intent of reducing manufacturing costs.[9]

Haring anticipated the cotton farmers' eventual demand for a mechanical picker and worked hard to provide them with an efficient machine. In 1916 some 25 years after he first began working on a cotton harvester, Haring patented and constructed yet another cotton picker. He designed this two-wheeled, horse-drawn machine to straddle a single row of cotton, and he incorporated the basic principles of his other models. Power was transmitted over a shaft between the wheels to an endless chain of slats. These slats rotated inward from front to rear at the same rate the picker moved forward. As the machine passed down a row, the corkscrew picking points gathered the cotton from the bolls. As with the other models, when the spindles reached the rear of the machine, the picking points automatically reversed direction, thereby releasing the cotton. A conveyor belt located on each side of the machine deposited the fiber into a detachable wooden hopper at the top of the cotton picker. The machine weighed about 1,000 pounds and could cover eight acres a day without damaging the cotton plant or reducing the grade of the cotton.[10]

For the next eight years, Haring improved his cotton picker but he did not succeed in demonstrating the ma-

Before IHC built a commercially viable picker in 1942, its engineers had experimented with hundreds of spindle designs. The spindles not only had to pick efficiently but also clean properly to prevent clogging. Ultimately, the IHC harvester used short, tapered, and slightly barbed spindles. (Courtesy of the Massie — Missouri Resources Division)

chine before representatives of the McCormick and International Harvester companies until October 1924. In a field north of Fort Worth, Texas, the machine picked 75 percent of the cotton the first time over the crop, and an additional 15 percent the second time. The picking points threw some cotton to the ground, but the loss was not appreciable. At the time of this demonstration, the cotton plants were in full foliage with green leaves, blooms, and unopened bolls. Even though the cotton picker apparently prevented trash from collecting in the cotton and provided a good sample, valued at the same price as hand-picked cotton, Haring still did not arouse sufficient interest among the officials present to win a contract.[11]

In early 1930, the *Progressive Farmer* reiterated the desire of many cotton farmers for a simple, dependable, and reasonably priced picker that could harvest the first crop of the season without damaging the plant for later picking. To enable widespread use of the machine, the picker would have to be attachable to either a team or a tractor and cost no more than a grain binder. Although the journal noted that such a machine was not yet available, it did give some publicity to the cotton picker which Haring patented in 1929, and described it as consisting of 100 spindles with 900 sets of revolving, curved picking fingers. This machine, with various technical adjustments, picked cotton by the same method as the 1916 model. An observer reported that under tests the machine did a good job of twisting the cotton from the bolls and releasing it

In November 1984, this John Deere diesel-powered cotton harvester, Model 699, picked the crop near Spring Hope, North Carolina. Self-propelled machines, such as this, harvested virtually the entire crop. (Courtesy of the Smithsonian Institution)

onto the conveyor belts. Unfortunately, the picking arms whipped through the branches and injured the plants.[12]

Either Haring or his supporters quickly corrected the *Progressive Farmer* and claimed the machine could pick 85 percent of the cotton without damaging the plants. Haring believed this model incorporated all the necessary features for commercial production — light weight, small size, moderate cost, and operating simplicity. He had great faith that his cotton picker merited commercial production, and he joined T. A. Kelly, a California investor, in organizing the Automatic Cotton Picker Company on 21 July 1930. Kelly believed he could raise $10,000 among investors to support production of the cotton picker. Although Kelly secured orders for 105 machines, he was unable to raise sufficient capital to make the company viable. Thus, when Haring believed he had finally reached the point of perfecting a marketable machine, the Great Depression ended his chance of securing sufficient funds to produce it.[13]

The Rust Harvester

In 1928 John D. Rust, a self-trained agricultural engi-

neer, together with his brother Mack, who held a degree in mechanical engineering from the University of Texas, also were at work on a machine which used smooth, wet spindles for picking. As early as 1924, Rust had experimented with a barbed or serrated spindle designed to twist the lint from the boll, and he achieved limited success similar to that which Haring experienced. This two-row machine, mounted on an Avery tricycle tractor, however, ultimately proved unsatisfactory. Although the barbs caught the cotton, the Rusts could not devise a method to remove the lint from the spindles. Then, three years later, John Rust remembered how the dew caused the cotton to stick to his fingers when he picked it during his boyhood, and that his grandmother moistened the spindle of her spinning wheel in order to get the cotton to adhere properly. Rust quickly designed a machine with an endless belt to which he attached vertical rows of dampened, smooth wire spindles that rotated against the cotton plants. Steel ribbons stripped the cotton from the spindles, and the machine then conveyed the lint to a storage basket. Rust filed patent papers for his cotton picker in 1928 and completed building his first test model that year. In 1931, near Waco, Texas, Rust's machine harvested a bale of cotton during the test day. Two years later, he had improved it to pick five bales per day at the Delta Experiment Station at Stoneville, Mississippi. In late August 1936, Rust's machine harvested 400 pounds or 4/5 bale in an hour at the Delta Experiment Station. The lint, however, had a large amount of trash in it, and the machine left much of the cotton in the bolls. Even so, this implement proved that mechanical harvesting was possible with a few improvements, because it picked at a rate of 40 to 50 times faster than hand pickers. The potential savings in labor were clearly apparent. In 1937 the Rust harvester picked at a rate of 13 bales per day without apparent difficulty. Financing, however, always remained a problem for the Rust brothers. By 1936, they had spent more than $50,000 for development of their cotton picker, and on the eve of World War II, their picker remained in the developmental stage with no prospect for commercial production.[14]

Even with these failures, cumulative knowledge and technological need were beginning to create the right circumstances for the final development of a mechanical cotton picker. Indeed, cotton farming hovered on the threshold of major technological change. Since the early twentieth century, cotton farmers had become increasingly interested in mechanization to offset rising costs and an uncertain labor supply. In 1914 the United States produced more than 16 million bales (weighing 600 pounds each) of cotton on nearly 37 million acres, or about two-thirds of the cotton marketed in the world. At that time, cotton farmers paid pickers 75 cents to $1 per 100 pounds of cotton while prices averaged only 60 cents to $1 per 100 pounds, depending on the season and location. With this delicate balance between costs and prices, an inadequate labor supply could bring financial ruin, if the crop could not be picked when it was ripe. During World

The cotton harvester was the most important technological hardware applied to Southern agriculture during the twentieth century. It helped eliminate thousands of jobs at picking time and contributed to the release of sharecroppers and tenant farmers. (Courtesy of the Smithsonian Institution)

War I, higher paying jobs lured Southern black workers to Northern cities, and schools sometimes closed to provide an adequate number of picking hands. Consequently, farmers began anticipating the development of a cotton picker that would solve their harvesting problems.[15]

Since a mechanical picker was not yet available, some Texas and Oklahoma farmers began hand snapping, then stripping their cotton crops. When cotton is snapped, the picker pulls the entire boll from the stalk rather than just picking the fiber from it. A special cleaner, known as a huller or boll extractor, was required to dislodge the heavier trash before the cotton passed through the gin. Not all of the trash could be removed, however, and snapping usually lowered the cotton two grades. Still, an average farm hand could snap about 50 percent more lint cotton per day than one could pick.[16]

Because farmers paid their pickers by poundage, however, workers were naturally careless about the amount of leaves, burs, and stalks they threw into the sack. Both snapping and sledding methods relied upon the cotton gin to remove the excess trash from the lint. Ginning, however, did not remove all the extra trash from the fiber and the foreign material interfered with the manufacture of yarns. Spinners also hesitated paying freight on snapped or sledded cotton, since not all of the weight was lint. As a result, cotton harvested by these methods often was reduced in grade, and the price declined accordingly. If the trash could be eliminated to the percentage present in hand-picked cotton, though, the grade and price were not materially affected.[17]

Cotton Strippers

In 1926, an exceptionally large cotton crop made snapping prohibitively slow and expensive, and southern Great Plains farmers turned to the cotton sled to speed the harvest. First patented by John Hughes of New Berne, North Carolina, on 28 March 1871, a cotton sled consisted of a wooden box on runners with wood or steel fingers set about one inch apart. The sled stripped the cotton from the stalks as the plants passed between the runners. These sleds could be made on the farm or by the local blacksmith for less than $30. Generally, one man and a team could sled six to seven times more cotton than an average hand could snap, or approximately four to five acres per day. Sledded cotton also required extra cleaning, but the cost of sledding, even with the loss of grade and dockage for excess trash, was considerably less than hand picking, averaging $2.78 per bale in 1926.[18]

Sleds were not suited for the heavier plants grown in the deep South, but on the southern Plains this harvesting method spread rapidly. The success of the cotton sled encouraged Deere & Company to develop a mechanical stripper which the firm tested near Plainview, Texas, in 1927. By late 1932, Deere produced 500 horse-drawn strippers annually for sale in Texas and Oklahoma. The Great Depression, however, ended this market when six-cent cotton, little cash for the purchase of new implements, and a large labor supply temporarily removed the need for a mechanical cotton harvester. Nevertheless, engineers at the Texas Agricultural Experiment Station at College Station continued to experiment with a mechanical stripper. By 1935 the station's engineers had developed a tractor-mounted, one-row stripper with a burr-extractor mounted on the rear of the tractor. This extractor helped clean the cotton as it was harvested. By 1940 mechanical strippers harvested about all of the cotton crop near Lubbock and approximately 95 percent of the crop in the vicinity of College Station. Over the next decade, agricultural engineers substituted fiber brushes for metal stripping teeth and added an air conveyor system. In 1949 farmers in the southern Great Plains mechanically stripped approximately 40 percent of the cotton crop; and, by the 1953 season, more than 18,000 strippers were ready for the harvest. As a result, another important step had been taken toward the complete mechanization of cotton farming.[19]

While agricultural implement companies tried to perfect a cotton stripper and picker, the Great Depression ironically provided the economic stimulus for the mechanization of Southern agriculture. With the Agricultural Adjustment Administration granting price supports for certain crops and paying farmers for taking cotton acreage out of production, many landowners preferred to receive guaranteed government payments rather than rental payments in the form of cotton from sharecroppers. Consequently, landlords released sharecroppers and used government checks to purchase tractors, milking machines, corn pickers, and combines. Bankrupt small farmers also sold their lands to more prosperous farmers. As a result, the agricultural work force declined and farm land became increasingly consolidated into larger operations which were more suitable, in terms of area and capital, for mechanization. Consequently, the need for hired labor and horses and mules declined still further.[20]

World War II

World War II provided another stimulus for the mechanization of Southern agriculture. During the war years, industrialization again lured many black farm workers to Northern and Southern cities. Indeed, between 1940 and 1950, the black farm population declined approximately 21 percent in the South, while the region's urban population increased 36 percent. Moreover, approximately 30 percent of the 12 million men and women who served in the armed forces were Southerners. Thus, between 1940 and 1950, migration and military service for blacks and whites decreased the Southern population by 20 percent, while the population of sharecroppers dropped 17.5 percent from 541,291 to 446,556. Southern landowners responded to this labor shortage by adopting more tractors, peanut pickers, hay balers, and dairy equipment. Since an affordable and reliable cotton picker was not yet available, however, cotton farmers abandoned marginal lands to ease the labor supply problem. As a result, cotton acreage declined by 5.5 million harvested acres between 1942 and 1945, even though the price of cotton increased from 17 cents to 22 cents per pound. Moreover, gasoline and rubber shortages severely limited the number of migratory workers available at picking time, particularly in the West.

For those workers who were available for the cotton harvest, wages more than tripled the previous level. Wages, for example, increased 311 percent between 1940 and 1945 as rates climbed from 62 cents to $1.93 per 100 pounds of seed cotton across the cotton belt. By 1948 pickers received $2.90 per 100 pounds of seed cotton for a 468 percent wage increase since 1940. With high wartime prices and soaring labor costs, cotton farmers wanted their crops harvested as quickly as possible, because cotton lost grade and price if it remained in the field for a long time after the bolls opened, and because speed reduced labor costs. For cotton farmers, then, a mechanical picker would enable a timely harvest and eliminate labor difficulties.[21]

International Harvester

While cotton farmers contended with their labor problems, agricultural engineers at the International Harvester Company worked to develop an efficient picker; and, in 1942, IHC emerged as the leader in the field of cotton harvesting technology. As early as January 1924, International Harvester purchased the Price-Campbell patents, and the company tested its first spindle picker that autumn. Over the next few years, IHC tested both self-propelled and tractor-drawn harvesters. These one-row, ground-wheel-powered pickers also proved unsatisfactory, because the machines brushed too much cotton onto the ground, damaged the plants, clogged, and bogged down in muddy fields. From 1926 to 1930, IHC simplified and improved the spindle picker by developing short, tapered, barbed spindles, and by applying Rust's principle of moistened spindles as well. These adjustments ulti-

In 1957, this two-row, John Deere Model 99 cotton harvester picked a field near Fresno, California. By the late 1950s, cotton pickers were readily affordable for those large-scale farmers who produced at least 100 bales annually. (Courtesy of the Deere & Company Archives)

In 1983, this John Deere 7449 self-propelled cotton stripper harvested six rows at once. Notice the low rate of cotton left in the foreground. Because the cotton stripper destroyed the plant, the crop had to be mature at harvest time. (Courtesy of the Deere & Company Archives)

mately proved successful.[22]

By mid-November 1942, International Harvester had developed a cotton picker that worked well enough to merit commercial sale. The machine consisted of two rotating drums with spindles approximately four inches long and one-fourth of an inch in diameter. The spindles were about four inches apart; and, as the drums rotated past a cotton plant the wetted spindles extracted the lint from the bolls. Rubber doffers removed the fibers from the spindles, and an air conveyor blew the cotton into an overhead container. A modified Farmall M tractor, operating in reverse, propelled the picker and powered the mechanisms of the implement. A continued farm labor shortage after World War II and additional technical improvements made the machine a commercial success. Production steadily increased; and, by 1949, about 1,500 spindle pickers were operating in the South and in California.[23]

Still, ginners graded mechanically harvested cotton lower than hand-picked cotton, because machine-picked cotton contained plant material. During the 1944 season, the Mississippi Delta Experiment Station produced hand-picked cotton which graded slightly above low-middling while mechanically picked cotton averaged slightly less than low-middling for a difference of 1.4 grades. The price was affected accordingly. From 1 September 1944 through 31 January 1945, hand-picked cotton sold for an average price of 21.73 cents per pound on the Memphis market. At that same time, the average price of machine-picked cotton was 18.05 cents per pound for a difference of 3.68 cents per pound or $18.40 per bale. Most cotton farmers, however, were prepared to absorb this loss, because cotton could deteriorate in grade even more if it was not picked at the correct time. Moreover, the cost of hand-picking a

1,600 pound bale of seed cotton averaged $36.76, while machine-picked cotton cost only $33.40 per bale for a savings of $3.36 per bale. In addition, the mechanical picker relieved the cotton farmer from the time-consuming task of hiring workers and from the expense of maintaining quarters for them. Some agricultural engineers also estimated that the man-hours required to raise one acre of cotton could be reduced by 65 percent, if mechanical cotton pickers were used with tractors and multiple-rowed planters and cultivators. In time, the grading problem was solved when spinners realized mechanically picked cotton was superior to hand-picked cotton. Mechanical pickers tended to extract the longer, stronger fibers while the shorter, weaker fibers were left in the bolls. Better dryers and cleaners also aided the ginning process and helped reduce the problem of grade loss for machine-picked cotton.[24]

Still, the cost of owning a cotton picker was high considering more than half of the cotton farmers planted fewer than 30 acres and produced less than four bales annually in the South. International Harvester's first commercial model sold for $5,985; and, when added to the cost of a Farmall M tractor on which it was mounted, the price soared to $7,600. Nevertheless, the commercial market for mechanical pickers quickly developed among cotton farmers who produced at least 100 bales per year. The implement companies gave major attention to cost reduction; and, by 1952, the International Harvester Company sold one model for $2,800. With this price decrease, and with John Deere selling a mechanical stripper for $905 as early as 1948, the technology became affordable for a completely mechanized cotton harvest. By the late 1960s, pickers and strippers harvested 96 percent of the cotton crop and helped reduced the man-hours required in the cotton fields from 122 to about 25 per acre. With each two-row implement replacing approximately 80 workers, and with the cotton crop fully mechanized, the cotton picker has eliminated at least one million men and women from harvest fields since the late 1940s.[25]

Social and Economic Costs

Technological change has not always met with approval, however, particularly from those whose jobs are threatened by it. In 1869, for example, John M. Horner lost a combine to fire in a California wheat field, probably set by a disgruntled harvest hand, and migrant workers also have objected to the use of mechanical tomato pickers. Although Southern sharecroppers, tenants, and day laborers did not rise up in opposition to the development of a mechanical cotton harvester, the Rust brothers recognized this innovation would cause great dislocation among the agricultural workers and other marginal farmers who lived from hand-to-mouth on the bottom of the social and economic ladder in the South. John Rust, who believed that his machine could do the work of 100 people in the fields, thought his picker would cause 75 percent of the sharecroppers to lose their tenuous hold on the land and force them into an even worse state of existence through unemployment.[26]

The Rust brothers knew that their cotton picker could improve Southern agriculture only if the implement could be mass produced and sold at an affordable price. Consequently, to help protect the sharecroppers, tenants, and day laborers who depended upon cotton farming, the Rust brothers designed their machine for the small-scale farmer. They believed it could be sold for less than $1,000, and that it could be powered by an all-purpose tractor with a power takeoff. They also hoped to market their machines with restrictions applied to the owner. First, they did not plan to sell their cotton pickers outright but only to lease them to farmers who agreed to pay minimum wages and to maintain maximum hours for their employees. Second, the Rusts also planned to prohibit farmers from leasing their machines if they did not abolish child labor on their properties. Although these ideas were commendable and clearly show the Rust brothers' deep belief in their obligation to society, each idea was impractical considering the cultural traditions and economic needs of Southern agriculture.[27]

The Rust brothers also hoped that farm cooperatives would purchase their cotton picker in order to make the harvesting tasks of their members easier while at the same time saving them the expense of individual purchases. Inadequate financing and organizational and racial problems, however, hindered the development of the cooperative movement in the South at that time, and the Rust brothers' plan never reached fruition. These problems had not been resolved by the time the Rusts abandoned their efforts to mass produce an efficient cotton picker on the eve of World War II.[28]

Since the time during which the Rust brothers wrestled with the ethical and moral implications of technological change, historians, economists, and agricultural engineers have continued to debate the effect of the mechanical cotton picker on the lowest echelon of farmers in the Deep South. Some have argued that technological progress cannot be stopped and that it must lead wherever new knowledge takes agricultural development. If social readjustment is required, then so be it, but the work to advance technological knowledge must not be stopped or even slowed. Others have argued the cotton harvester did not push sharecroppers, tenants, and day laborers off the land so much as the lure of higher paying jobs in the cities pulled that class of farm workers from the countryside. The economists in this latter group argue that until 1957, the cost of picking cotton by hand was cheaper than picking it mechanically, and that farmers in the South did not completely mechanize the cotton harvest until 1975.[29]

Indeed, agricultural labor costs were cheaper in the South than in Arizona and California, where cotton also was an important crop, and where environmental conditions, such as dry weather during the harvest season, reduced the costs of mechanical harvesting and encouraged the use of cotton pickers. Consequently, mechanization first became established in the West, then moved to the South. In 1949, for example, the cost of hand-picking cotton in the Deep South averaged $2.28 per hundredweight and $2.60 per hundredweight in the Mid-South, whereas it cost $2.93 per hundredweight in the Far West. At the same time, the custom rates for machine harvesting the cotton crop averaging $3.80 and $3.00 per hundredweight in the Deep and Mid-South respectively, while that cost dropped to $2.50 per 100 pounds in the Far West. By 1957, however, mechanical harvesting costs had dropped below hand labor expenses in the South. In that year, the cost of hand picking in the Deep South averaged $2.66 per hundredweight and $2.73 per hundredweight in the Mid-South. The cost in the Far West averaged $3.18 per 100 pounds. In contrast, the cost of mechanical picking averaged $2.50 per hundredweight in the Deep South and $2.00 in the Mid-South while it dropped to 50 cents per hundredweight in the Far West. Thereafter, the cost of mechanical picking remained lower than hand picking in both the South as well as the Far West. Although the differences in cost between hand- and machine-picked cotton are important for stimulating or retarding technological change, the analysis of these costs alone places too much emphasis on the influence of the cotton picker and not enough importance on the tractor's reduction of the preharvest labor force. As a result, one can easily overlook another important technological "push" on the agricultural labor force in the South.[30]

Not everyone, of course, agrees with this assessment. Some contend that the slowness to adopt the cotton picker in the South reflects the influence of cultural institutions, such as small-scale production and the propensity of plantation owners to use annual labor contracts to guarantee an adequate number of tenants and sharecroppers throughout the crop year. Still others charged that inadequate capital, insufficient financing, and the absence of preharvest mechanization slowed the adoption of cotton pickers in the South. Certainly, in California cultural institutions, large-scale farms, environmental conditions, and an uncertain labor supply made mechanization far easier than in the South. In California, high yields produced by the intensive use of fertilizer and irrigation encouraged mechanization. There, cotton farmers did not need so many workers for weeding the crop as did the Southern planters. The dry climate permitted the use of tractors and cultivators to keep the weeds under control. Fewer weeds meant their cotton pickers were less likely to fill the lint with trash. Farmers in California also harvested more acres than did cotton farmers in the South, thereby increasing the economy of scale and making mechanical pickers more affordable. In 1949, for example, the average cotton farm in California produced 103 acres while the average farm in South Carolina raised about 13 acres of cotton. At that time, economists determined that cotton farmers needed at least 100 acres to make the purchase of a cotton picker feasible. By that time, however, three-fourths of the cotton farmers in California harvested more than 100 acres. Cotton farmers in California also adopted the tractor more readily than did farmers in the South. By 1950, for example, farmers in California were more than four times as likely to use a tractor than were farmers in Mississippi. Thus, by the time the cotton picker became technologically feasible, farmers in California already had made a major commitment to technological change.[31]

In California, moreover, seasonal, migrant workers customarily harvested the cotton crop, rather than a peasant class of sharecroppers and tenants that characterized Southern agriculture. In California, the peak labor season came at harvest time for the cotton crop, because tractors essentially had mechanized the other phases of cotton production. In the South, however, the preharvest preparation of the land and crop dominated the planter's attention in relation to agricultural labor. Consequently, periodic scarcity of labor at harvest time, as well as the cost savings by harvesting mechanically, stimulated farmers in California to adopt the cotton picker. Indeed, among 63 growers in the San Joaquin Valley, who used mechanical cotton pickers in 1949, the cost of harvesting a bale of cotton averaged $28.12 compared to $45 per bale for hand picking for a savings of $16.88 per bale. In contrast, Southern cotton farmers faced mechanical-picking costs of approximately $15 to $20 per bale higher than those incurred in California. This average, of course, is determined in part by the number of acres planted and the yields returned. Moreover, larger acreages of the cotton crop decreased the cost of mechanical harvesting, but not for hand picking.[32]

Plant breeders also were able to change the plant sooner in California than in the South to help farmers mechanize. In California, they shortened the growing season by as much as 30 days to permit harvesting before the onset of wet autumn weather, and they raised the bolls by four inches to reduce the tendency of the mechanical harvester to collect dirt and weeds. Agricultural scientists also discovered the advantages of closely spacing the plants to facilitate machine picking and developed defoliants to reduce the plant material on the stalks at harvest time. Moreover, an efficient extension service spread the knowledge about the benefits of mechanized harvesting throughout California's cotton-producing region. As a result, California led all other states in the mechanical picking of cotton, and it became the first state to mechanize fully the cotton harvest.[33]

Conclusion

In retrospect, with the perfection of the mechanical harvester, farmers could completely mechanize their cotton crop, if they could afford to do so. Mechanization saved time and money and eliminated the problems caused by an uncertain labor supply. At the same time, mechanical cotton harvesters have contributed to the consolidation of small-scale farms into larger holdings. In 1950, for example, 304,469 farms raised cotton as the major crop, but farmers only harvested 5 percent of the crop mechanically, mostly in California and Arizona. By 1974, the number of cotton farms had decreased to 89,500, and the crop essentially had been mechanized. The number of cotton farms dropped still further to 43,046 by 1987, on which 42,914 pickers and strippers harvested the crop. This decline was due in part to the growth of the synthetic fiber industry. By 1988, for example, clothing manufacturers used only three billion pounds of cotton for approximately 27 percent of their fiber. At the same time they used eight billion pounds of synthetic fiber for nearly 72 percent of their needs.[34]

Certainly, the development of a successful cotton picker did not come easily. Some inventors failed to produce an efficient cotton harvester because they only vaguely perceived the importance of the changing sources of farm power. During the 1920s, the Farmall tractor permitted rapid progress in the preharvest stage of cotton farming. While Haring, for example, ultimately admitted that his cotton picker did not harvest enough cotton, he attributed the fault to insufficient draft power. He believed the mere conversion from horse to tractor power would solve the problem. This assumption was a crucial mistake, because the cotton picker, even though tractor-pulled, still functioned on the power transmitted from the ground wheels. Had Haring redesigned the cotton picker to operate from the tractor's power takeoff, he would have attained a more constant and reliable picking speed and perhaps improved picking efficiency.[35]

The inherent characteristics of the cotton plant as it existed at that time also posed problems for the development of a universally acceptable mechanical picker. Because the cotton bolls did not ripen uniformly and because the early opened cotton deteriorated rapidly if it was left unpicked, a farmer could not wait until all of the bolls opened to harvest his crop. The height of the plants also varied in the fields as well as between geographical regions, thus requiring machine adaptability to plants ranging from a few inches to several feet high a necessity. In 1927, the development of a cotton plant that matured early and produced bolls in clusters on short stems, a development which would facilitate mechanical harvesting, was only in the experimental stage for Southern agriculture.[36]

The development of a marketable cotton harvester also required the resolution of certain technical and economic problems. The machine had to be reasonably priced, and simple to operate and repair. It had to maneuver on moderately rough terrain and in muddy fields. It had to possess sufficient carrying capacity to make unloading in mid-row unnecessary. And, it had to pick a high percentage of cotton without trash or damage to the lint. In addition, chemical defoliants and weed killers had to be developed to help eliminate the problem of trash in the machine-harvested fiber. Only when scientists and agricultural engineers mastered these problems did a cotton picker have belt-wide appeal in the South. Ultimately, the cumulative contributions of mechanical engineers, plant breeders, and chemists made the development of the cotton picker possible by the early 1940s.[37]

Few inventors could afford the time, money, or the commitment to develop a successful cotton picker. Only a major implement company, with millions of dollars and many engineers, could make such an investment with any hope of success. In 1942, after nearly 40 years of research at an estimated cost of $5,250,000, the International Harvester Company demonstrated the first satisfactory cotton picker, but it manufactured only 52 machines from 1942 to 1945 and only 300 machines by 1947, although total sales reached 1,500 implements a year later. Further improvements would come only with time.[38]

Still, the basic ideas which led to the mechanization of the cotton harvest came from individual inventors, such as Campbell, Rust, and Price. Many of these agricultural engineers and tinkerers were field-testing their inventions at the same time and, with the exception of Rust, they probably were familiar with the failures and successes of their counterparts. Each inventor hoped his work would resolve the most perplexing bottleneck in cotton farming. The task, however, was simply too much for one man, who had to rely upon benefactors, family, friends, and economically shaky self-made companies for financial support. Nevertheless, each inventor contributed to the eventual perfection of a mechanical picker, even if he only showed which lines of development were unproductive. By so doing, each helped solve the most important regional problem involving technological change in American agriculture.

NOTES

1. James H. Street, *The New Revolution in the Cotton Economy* (Chapel Hill: University of North Carolina Press, 1957), 92-93, 107; Frank J. Welch, "Mechanization of the Cotton Harvest," *Journal of Farm Economics*, 27 (Nov. 1945): 932-933. By the term agricultural engineer, I am referring to professionally trained mechanical engineers who were employed by implement companies, state experiment stations, or land-grand universities to develop new technology for agriculture. They may or may not have been members of the American Society of Agricultural Engineers which was founded in 1907.

2. Street, *The New Revolution in the Cotton Economy*, 107-108.

3. *Ibid.*, 108-110.

4. *Ibid.*, 107-108, 111.

5. *Ibid.*, 117-118; John Jewkes, *The Sources of Invention* (New York: St. Martin's Press, 1959), 283.

6. William Deering & Company to P. P. Haring, 17 Sept. 1891, and 25 June 1895, Haring Manuscript Collection, National Museum of American History, Smithsonian Institution (hereafter SI). *Annual Report of the Commissioner of Patents, 1897* (Washington: Government Printing Office, 1898), 152, 524; Patent Specification Letters, no. 587, 201, 1897.

7. R. B. Swift, McCormick Harvesting Machine Company, Chicago, to Haring, 8 and 15 Nov., 6 Dec. 1897, and 31 Mar. 1898, SI.

8. *Annual Report of the Commissioner of Patents, 1905* (Washington: Government Printing Office, 1906), 192, 729; Patent Specification Letters, no. 796,421, 8 Aug. 1905.

9. "Articles of Incorporation of the Haring Cotton Machine Company," SI; *Annual Report of the Commissioner of Patents, 1911* (Washington: Government Printing Office, 1912), 209, 717; Patent Specification Letters, no. 588, 184, 23 May 1911; *Annual Report of the Commissioner of Patents, 1913* (Washington: Government Printing Office, 1914), 208, 733; Patent Specification Letters, no. 1,054,113, 25 Feb. 1913, and no. 1,076,573, 21 Oct. 1913.

10. *Annual Report of the Commissioner of Patents, 1916* (Washington, D.C.: Government Printing Office, 1917), 267, 945; Patent Specification Letters, no. 1,176,891, 28 Mar. 1916; "A Machine That Picks Cotton Without Injuring the Plant," *Scientific American*, 114 (Jan.-June 1916): 551, 564; "A Practical Automatic Cotton Picker," SI; "Declares Cotton Picking Machine Perfected," newspaper clipping (n.p., n.d.), SI.

11. "Field Demonstration," SI.

12. *Progressive Farmer*, 8 Feb. 1930; 4, 8, 30, and 29 Mar. 1930, 4; *Index of Patents Issued from the United States Patent Office, 1929* (Washington, D.C.: Government Printing Office, 1930), 294, 848; Patent Specification Letters, no. 1,715, 655, 4 June 1929.

13. *Progressive Farmer*, 29 Mar. 1930, 4; Patent Specification Letters no. 1,715,665, 4 June 1929; "The Wonder Machine of the Cotton Seed World," SI; T. A. Kelly to Haring, 26 July 1930, 21 Jan. and 11 Aug. 1931, 3 Feb. 1932, SI.

14. Street, *The New Revolution in the Cotton Economy*, 123-125; John Rust, "The Origin and Development of the Cotton Picker," *West Tennessee Historical Society Papers*, 7 (1953 reprint): 9-15.

15. *Historical Statistics of the United States from Colonial Times to 1957* (Washington, D.C.: Government Printing Office, 1960), 301; "A Machine That Picks Cotton," 551; *Dallas News*, 2 Dec. 1917.

16. "White Gold," Cotton Machine Corporation, Fort Worth, TX (n.d.), 4; A. P. Brodell and M. R. Cooper, "Requirements and Costs for Picking, Snapping, and Sledding Cotton in Western Texas and Oklahoma," USDA, Bureau of Agricultural Economics (Washington, D.C., June 1927), 1-2, National Agricultural Library; M. E. Campbell and H. H. Willis, "Spinning Test of Picked and Snapped Cotton," USDA, Bureau of Agricultural Economics (Washington, D.C., June 1928), 1, 10-11, National Agricultural Library; Street, *The New Revolution in the Cotton Economy*, 112-113.

17. "IHC to Make Cotton Harvesting Machine," *Farm Implement News — Chicago* (n.d.), 24; Campbell, "Spinning Test of Picked and Snapped Cotton," 1, 10-12; *Dallas Morning News*, 10 Aug. 1932; Patent Specification Letters, no. 1,768, 837, 1 July 1930.

18. Street, *The New Revolution in the Cotton Economy*, 112; Brodell, "Requirements and Costs for Picking, Snapping, and Sledding Cotton in Western Texas and Oklahoma," 2, 4, 6-7; "IHC to Make Cotton Harvesting Machines," 24.

19. Street, *The New Revolution in the Cotton Economy*, 113-115; P. H. Stephens, "Mechanization of Cotton Farms," *Journal of Farm Economics*, 13 (Jan. 1931): 35; Gilbert C. Fite, "Recent Progress in the Mechanization of Cotton Production in the United States," *Agricultural History*, 24 (Jan. 1950): 24.

20. Pete Daniel, "The Transformation of the Rural South 1930 to the Present," *Agricultural History*, 55 (July 1981): 236, 243-245; Pete

20. Pete Daniel, "The Transformation of the Rural South 1930 to the Present," *Agricultural History*, 55 (July 1981): 236, 243-245; Pete Daniel, *Breaking the Land: The Transformation of Cotton, Tobacco, and Rice Cultures Since 1880* (Urbana: University of Illinois, 1985), 244; Warren C. Whatley, "Labor for the Picking: The New Deal in the South," *Journal of Economic History*, 43 (Dec. 1983): 905-929.

21. Richard S. Kirkendall, "Up to Now: A History of American Agriculture from Jefferson to Revolution to Crisis," *Agriculture and Human Values*, 4 (Winter 1987): 10; *Historical Statistics of the United States*, 457, 465, 517; Street, *The New Revolution in the Cotton Economy*, 179-205, 239.

22. Harris P. Smith, "Late Developments in Mechanical Cotton Harvesting," *Agricultural Engineering*, 27 (July 1946): 321; Fite, "Recent Progress in the Mechanization of Cotton Production," 25-26; C. R. Hagan, "Twenty-Five Years of Cotton Picker Development," *Agricultural Engineering*, 32 (Nov. 1951): 595; Gilbert C. Fite, "Mechanization of Cotton Production Since World War II," *Agricultural History*, 54 (Jan. 1980): 194-195.

23. Street, *The New Revolution in the Cotton Economy*, 120-122, 130; Hagan, "Twenty-Five Years of Cotton Picker Development," 593-596; Fite, "Recent Progress in the Mechanization of Cotton Production," 26; Fite, "Mechanization of Cotton Production Since World War II," 194-195.

24. Frank J. Welch and D. Gray Miley, "Mechanization of the Cotton Harvest," *Journal of Farm Economics*, 27 (Nov. 1945): 936, 939-940, 943; Smith, "Late Developments in Mechanical Cotton Harvesting," 321; Rex F. Colwick and Vernon P. Moore, "King Cotton Blasts Off," *Yearbook of Agriculture, 1970*, 45.

25. Fite, "Recent Progress in the Mechanization of Cotton Production," 27; Street, *The New Revolution in the Cotton Economy*, 115; Fite, "Mechanization of Cotton Production Since World War II," 202-203; Colwick and Moore, "King Cotton Blasts Off," 40-42.

26. Street, *The New Revolution in the Cotton Economy*, 126; R. Douglas Hurt, *American Farm Tools: From Hand-Power to Steam-Power* (Manhattan, KS: Sunflower University Press, 1982), 80.

27. Street, *The New Revolution in the Cotton Economy*, 126-127.

28. *Ibid.*

29. Willis Peterson and Yoav Kislev, "The Cotton Harvester in Retrospect: Labor Displacement or Replacement?" *Journal of Economic History*, 46 (Mar. 1986): 199-201, 205.

30. *Ibid.*, 207; Warren C. Whatley, "Southern Agrarian Labor Contracts as Impediments to Cotton Mechanization," *Journal of Economic History*, 47 (Mar. 1987): 63.

31. Whatley, "Southern Agrarian Labor Contracts," 45; Gilbert C. Fite, *Cotton Fields No More: Southern Agriculture, 1865-1980* (Lexington: University of Kentucky Press, 1984), 150, 185-188; Moses S. Musoke and Alan L. Olmstead, "The Rise of the Cotton Industry in California: A Comparative Perspective," *Journal of Economic History*, 43 (June 1982): 385-386, 389, 391, 394-395, 402-403.

32. Musoke and Olmstead, "The Rise of the Cotton Industry in California," 395-397, 400, 401, 402-403, 409.

33. *Ibid.*, 404-405.

34. Fite, "Mechanization of Cotton Production Since World War II," 204-207; *1982 Census of Agriculture*, 8: 9; *Agricultural Statistics, 1987*, 61; Fite, *Cotton Fields No More*, 185-186; *1987 Census of Agriculture*, I: 8, 18; *Statistical Abstract of the United States, 1988*, 720.

35. Fite, "Recent Progress in the Mechanization of Cotton Production," 21; "IHC to Make Cotton Harvesting Machines," 24; Haring to J. I. Case Company, 28 Mar. 1935, SI; J. D. Lecr, Assistant to the Secretary, Department of Agriculture, Washington, D.C., to Haring, 26 May 1935, SI.

36. Arthur P. Chew, "Cheaper Cotton Picking," *Farm Journal*, 51 (Aug. 1927): 12; H. P. Smith, "Cotton Harvesting Development to Date," *Agricultural Engineering*, 12 (Mar. 1935): 77-78.

37. M. G. Vardin, J. O. Smith, and W. E. Ayres, "Making Cotton Cheaper: Can Present Production Costs Be Reduced?" Mississippi Delta Experiment Station, *Bulletin No. 290* (Feb. 1931), 22-24; Street, *The New Revolution in the Cotton Economy*, 103; E. J. Gettins, J. I. Case Company, to Haring, 14 Oct. 1932, SI; Fite, "Mechanization of Cotton Production Since World War II," 191-192; Fite, *Cotton Fields No More*, 187.

38. Fite, "Recent Developments in the Mechanization of Cotton Production," 25; Street, *The New Revolution in the Cotton Economy*, 118, 120, 130, 132-133; Fite, *Cotton Fields No More* 185; Daniel, *Breaking the Land*, 246.

Chapter 3

Combine Harvesters

NOT long after Cyrus Hall McCormick and Obed Hussey patented their reapers in the early 1830s, and about the same time the Pitts brothers experimented with their thresher cleaner, Hiram Moore built the first successful combine, which he patented on 28 June 1836. The combine, however, did not become practical for small-scale farmers in the Midwest for nearly a century. Essentially, the combine is simply a combination of a reaper or harvester with a threshing machine attached.

Moore's combine, for example, was a huge threshing machine, mounted on wheels, with a reciprocating sickle and a gathering reel. This combine was 17 feet long and 15 feet wide. Two wheels, seven feet in diameter, with iron spikes to prevent slipping on wet ground, provided the power for the cutting and threshing mechanisms. A dividing bar on the edge of the machine separated the standing grain from that which was about to be cut. The sickle and reel were adjustable to permit cutting grain of various heights. The cutter bar consisted of a fixed plate with saw teeth and a saw-tooth sickle which oscillated on top. The cutter adjusted to permit shearing the heads close to the top of the stalk because the height of the grain varied from field to field or even within the same acreage. A gathering cylinder measured 4 feet in diameter and 12 feet in length. Rows of six-inch wooden or metal teeth extended from the cylinder. These teeth caught the grain and pulled it into the reciprocating sickle. An apron carried the cut grain to the threshing cylinder. Behind the cylinder a revolving wire riddle separated the straw and dropped it onto the ground. The threshed grain and chaff fell through a sieve where a winnowing fan blew away the chaff. The grain then passed through a conveyor and spout into bags. At least six men were required to operate Moore's combine. One rider also manned each four-horse team, while several additional workers hauled the grain sacks to the barn or granary. Moore's combine required 20 horses for draft.[1]

Although Hiram Moore believed that he had built a practical combine by 1843, capable of harvesting 25 acres per day, he continued to make improvements on his machine. By the late 1840s, Moore had changed the combine's design so that a huge, barrel-like threshing cylinder sat at an angle behind the reel. The separated straw dropped to the ground from the cylinder's open end. The grain fell through a screen at the bottom where a fan winnowed the chaff. The cleaned grain collected in a bin from which an elevator raised it to a platform where a worker, riding on the machine, collected it in bags. Sixteen horses, walking two abreast, pulled this machine which cut a ten-foot swath, and sacked the grain at the rate of 25 acres per day. Moore's combine worked best in fields free of stumps and large rocks, and it reportedly was simple enough for operation by "any man of ordinary common

During the early twentieth century, horse-drawn combines harvested the wheat crop on the large-scale farms in California and the Pacific Northwest. Note the gasoline engine and exhaust pipe on the front of the Case combine. This engine powered the combine, while the horses and mules pulled it forward, *ca.* 1917. (Courtesy of the Smithsonian Institution)

Corn for Grain or Seed: 1987

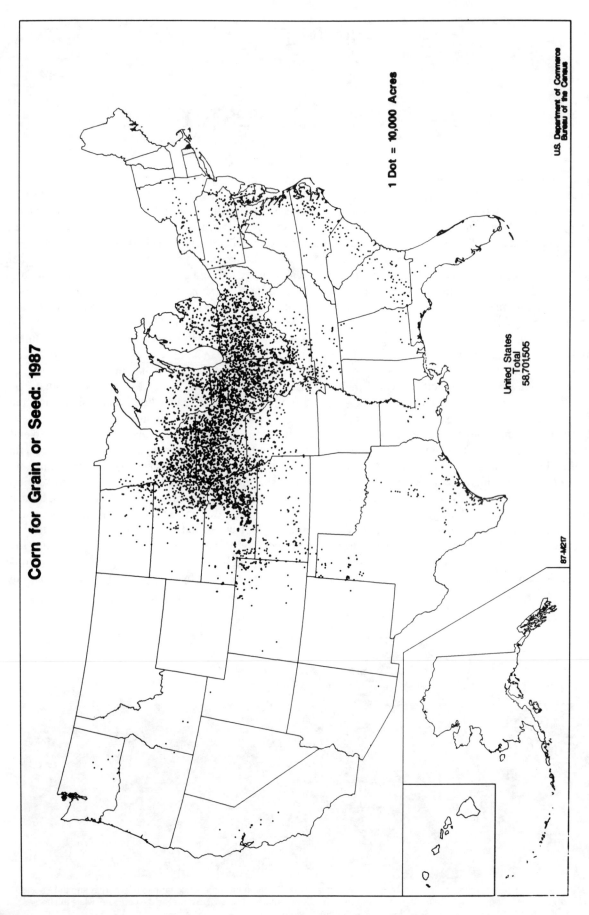

1 Dot = 10,000 Acres

United States
Total
58,701,505

87-M217

U.S. Department of Commerce
Bureau of the Census

The corn belt stretches across the Midwest from Ohio to the eastern edge of the Great Plains. Rich soil, favorable climate, and technology enabled farmers in this region to specialize in corn production. Deere & Company became the first implement manufacturer to design a corn head that could be fitted on a combine. Combines that cut and threshed corn, however, required more power and a stronger chassis than implements designed for harvesting small grains.

sense after two day's experience."[2]

Moore continued to make adjustments on his combine, but the Midwestern farmer did not adopt it, and it was not manufactured by any agricultural implement company. Four major problems prevented the acceptance of Moore's combine in the Midwestern grain belt. First, the fields were small, and Moore's combine was large, clumsy, and difficult to maneuver. The lighter, simpler, more manageable reapers just coming on the market required only two horses for draft instead of 16 or 20, and they were far more suitable for the grain farmer's needs. Second, the humid climate and wet summer weather of the Midwest kept the grain stalks from drying. Damp stalks and tough grain heads did not thresh properly and often clogged the cylinder. If a farmer cut his grain with a reaper and placed it in shocks, however, the grain dried sufficiently for machine threshing. Third, rain could delay the harvest for days or weeks, if the ground was too muddy for the combine to operate properly. While a farmer waited to get his combine into the field, more severe weather might destroy the entire crop. Fourth, Moore estimated that his combine would cost $500, far more than the Midwestern grain farmer could afford.[3]

Midwestern farmers weighed the disadvantage of Moore's combine against the advantage of quick completion of the harvest by cutting, threshing, and winnowing in one operation. Virtually all of them decided the risks of breakdowns, bad weather, and the expense of a machine that required far more draft horses than most farmers owned made the combine economically impractical. Eventually, Midwestern farmers would adopt the combine, but not for another half-century. Small combines, technologically suitable for Midwestern fields and crops, would reach the market at the start of the twentieth century. In the meantime, the header, binder, and threshing machine satisfied harvesting needs. Until after 1900, improvements in combine technology were designed to meet the needs of large-scale wheat farmers in California, Oregon, and Washington.

The Twentieth Century

Indeed, at the turn of the twentieth century, farmers still primarily used the combine only along the West Coast. Soon thereafter, however, farm implement manufacturers began to develop small, horse-drawn combines that cut a seven- to ten-foot swath. World War I stimulated these efforts and encouraged farmers to adopt combines by raising grain prices and reducing the labor supply. About 1917, Great Plains farmers began to purchase 12- to 16-foot combines, powered by an auxiliary gasoline engine mounted on the harvester. Tractors or horses still pulled these combines, but the auxiliary power source which drove the cutting and threshing mechanisms of the machine provided consistent and uniform power which could not be achieved from a ground wheel characteristic of the previous combine harvesters. The collapse of the farm economy in 1920, however, prevented immediate wide-scale adoption of this new harvesting implement which cost between $2,000 and $3,000. But farmers did begin to use the combine on a wide scale in the mid-1920s. Within ten years of that time, hard winter wheat farmers on the southern Great Plains harvested approximately 50 percent of their crop with combines, most of which had 12-foot cutter bars.[4]

By the mid-1920s, farmers in Texas, Oklahoma, Kansas, Nebraska, and Montana primarily used the combine. These farmers already had made the commitment to mechanization with their adoption of the tractor. Within a selected study area for each state, most farmers owned at least one tractor while about 50 percent used a motor truck. Several farmers operated entirely with mechanical power. Consequently, they did not resist other forms of mechanical power that would help them complete their grain harvest more quickly, efficiently, and cheaply than ever before.[5]

These early combines essentially remained headers with a threshing machine attached. A horse-drawn wagon followed along one side of the implement and caught the grain that fell from an elevated spout. Accessory equipment, which cost extra, included extensions for the cutter bar, straw spreaders, straw bunchers, and grain tanks. In the Great Plains, however, farmers usually did not save the wheat straw for feed, because it had low nutritional value, and they did not need great quantities of straw for livestock bedding. Moreover, the straw from the combine was not heavy enough to interfere with autumn plowing. Consequently, these farmers had little use for straw bunchers and instead used combines with straw spreaders. The combines with 15- and 16-foot cutter bars usually had straw spreaders included as standard equipment.[6]

By the mid-1920s, 30- to 60-bushel grain tanks had become a standard feature of the combine. Many farmers also attached grain tanks to their older implements. On hilly land, where the soil was loose, or where the tractor did not provide sufficient power for adequate draft, however, farmers sometimes had to remove the grain tank and substitute a horse-drawn wagon, pulled alongside, to ease the burden on the tractor. Even so, rolling land or fields with sandy soil often prevented the tractor from transferring sufficient power with a ground wheel to maintain a uniform speed for the combine's threshing cylinder. Farmers who owned larger combines sometimes circumvented this problem by adding an additional team of horses or by using a second tractor. Smaller machines did not permit adaptations such as these, and this problem would not be solved until auxiliary engines or power takeoff systems provided sufficient power for the moving parts of the combine. Combines with auxiliary engines and a 12-foot cutter bar usually required tractors with at least 15-horsepower for draft.[7]

Economic Need

Farmers remained interested in combines, because these implements, in part, could reduce their labor costs.

The J. I. Case Threshing Machine Company designed this horse-drawn combine for the small-scale farmer in the Midwest. The gasoline engine powered the machine. By the mid-1920s, the grain tank had become a standard feature on new combines. (Courtesy of the Parks Library, Iowa State University)

This Case combine was the first to leave the assembly line. By 1934, when this photograph was taken, it had harvested wheat near Hardtner, Kansas, since 1923. The tractor and driver are visible beyond the reel. The combine's operator steered from the rear and controlled the height of the sickle and reel. (Courtesy of the Smithsonian Institution)

During the 1920s, farmers on the Great Plains began using combines. With a 12- to 15-foot cutter bar and a 30- to 60-bushel grain tank, only three people were needed at harvest time — the tractor driver, combine operator, and truck driver. (Courtesy of the Smithsonian Institution)

In 1927, Deere & Company began combine production with the No. 2. This combine was ideally suited for farmers on the Great Plains. At the end of the decade combines harvested approximately 75 percent of the winter wheat crop in that region. (Courtesy of the Deere & Company Archives)

Indeed, during the early twentieth century, labor costs required major expenditures at harvest time. Prior to the adoption of the combine, wheat farmers customarily doubled their labor force for the harvest. Without a doubt, a timely and profitable harvest depended upon a wheat farmer's ability to secure adequate help at reasonable prices. The annual scarcity of harvest and threshing hands, however, drove labor prices upward and forced farmers to rely upon itinerant workers, because the rural neighborhoods and nearby small towns usually could not furnish an adequate number of hands. Labor shortages particularly were common in areas where large-scale farmers predominated and where they drew upon the same labor pool during harvest time. In the central part of the wheat belt farmers needed more than 100,000 harvest hands each year. Consequently, a combine crew that required four men, including two haulers, lessened a farmer's problem of finding workers and reduced his expenses because

headers usually required at least a six-man crew, while binders required one man to drive the tractor and one to shock. This harvesting procedure, however, still left the grain for threshing, and threshing brought additional expenses. In 1921, for example, a Great Plains farmer who hired "contract threshers," usually found that his labor costs ranged from $86 to $116 per day, or roughly from $3 to $5 per day for each worker.[8]

With a tractor and combine, a farmer no longer required hired help to gather the binder's sheaves into shocks and a crew to operate the threshing machine. At most, the farmer needed one man to drive the tractor, another to ride the combine, operate the cutter bar, and monitor the gasoline engine, and one to haul the threshed grain to a storage bin or grain elevator. If a farmer had sons, he did not need to hire help, and his labor costs could be absorbed by the family. By the mid-1920s, however, if a farmer required help at harvest time, he could expect to pay $5 to

Combines saved labor expenses during harvest time for large-scale farmers, but agriculturists with less than 125 acres of wheat could not afford that technological investment. By the mid-1920s, Great Plains farmers believed they needed nearly 300 acres of wheat to merit purchase of a combine. (Courtesy of the Smithsonian Institution)

In July 1929, this Rumely No. 3 combine harvested wheat near Bushton, Kansas. Rumely's tractor-drawn, gasoline engine-powered combine could harvest 15 bushels of wheat per acre at the rate of 1-acre every 45 minutes. (Courtesy of Thomas D. Isern)

$6 per day for a combine operator and from $4 to $6 per day for a tractor driver while haulers averaged $4 per day. Still, even when hired hands were necessary, the combine saved time and, as a result, money. If a wheat field, for example, averaged 15 bushels per acre, 4.6 man-hours were required to bind, shock, and thresh it. A similar crop required 3.8 man-hours to harvest with a header. In contrast, only .75 man-hours per acre were needed to harvest that grain with a combine.[9]

When all other costs are included, such as fuel and repairs, a farmer who used a 15-foot combine could cut an acre of grain for $1.50 while others expended $4.22 per acre for harvesting the crop with a binder and $3.36 per acre when using a header. Put differently, harvesting expenses averaged 10 cents per bushel when a farmer used a combine compared to 28 cents per bushel with a binder and 22 cents per bushel with a header. Farmers also made similar savings by using the combine instead of the binder

In 1925, the Advance-Rumely Thresher Company began building combines. Two years later, these custom cutters used Rumely models No. 1 and No. 2, together with two Rumley tractors near Duquine, Kansas. With a 20-foot reel or header, each combine could harvest 80 acres per day under the best conditions. (Courtesy of Thomas D. Isern)

to harvest grain sorghum in the southern and central Great Plains.[10]

Not every farmer, however, needed a combine to save money during the grain harvest. In fact, unless a wheat farmer on the Great Plains had at least 100 acres to cut during the mid-1920s, a ten-foot combine did not merit the investment. With custom cutters, who used a combine, charging an average of $3 per acre, small-scale farmers, with less than a quarter section in wheat, were most economical when they hired someone else to harvest their crop. Similarly, a farmer who owned a 15-foot combine needed at least 100 acres to warrant that investment, otherwise his costs would be less with a binder. Many wheat farmers on the Great Plains, however, believed that they needed even more acreage in grain than these estimates by the United States Department of Agriculture. They contended that a ten-foot combine, with a power takeoff, required at least 196 acres of wheat at harvest time to be profitable. They also argued that a 15-foot, tractor-drawn combine, which operated with an auxiliary engine,

needed 276 acres of wheat to cut before it merited the investment.[11]

Farmers who could afford the investment, however, willingly spent about $2,000 for combines during the mid-1920s, even though projections indicated these machines only would last about eight years. While this cost could be prohibitive, combines collected more grain than any other harvesting method. This advantage translated into more money at the elevator. On the average, during the mid-1920s, combines lost only 2.63 percent of the grain. In contrast, headers lost 3.27 percent while binders proved the most wasteful of all, averaging 6.06 percent losses. These comparisons are based on similar harvesting conditions and an average yield of 20.4 bushels per acre. Put differently, these losses averaged 32 pounds per acre for combines and 40 and 74 pounds per acre, respectively, for headers and binders. Combines, however, did not thresh as much grain as the stationary separators or "thrashing" machines powered by gasoline tractors or steam engines, but these differences were negligible be-

This Holt combine manufactured in Stockton, California, used a power takeoff to operate the implement, thereby, eliminating the need for an auxiliary gasoline engine. Combines, such as this, were well suited for small fields, but farmers needed nearly 200 acres of wheat to make this implement affordable. (Courtesy of the Parks Library, Iowa State University)

Many small-scale farmers used the John Deere Model B tractor and combine with a power takeoff connection on their grain crops. The six-foot reel and small grain tank had little capacity, but the combine saved time and labor costs on this Missouri farm, *ca.* 1940. (Courtesy of the State Historical Society of Missouri)

cause combines lost only 1.9 percent of the grain during separation while threshing machines lost 1.2 percent.[12]

The combine's savings in grain and labor encouraged many wheat farmers on the Great Plains to purchase these implements. Many farmers believed they could pay for their combine in one year, or, at worst, after a "short time," if they could cut enough wheat. In 1925, for example, combines could harvest wheat for about five cents per bushel, based on labor and implement costs for an average crop. In contrast, threshermen charged as much as 18 cents per bushel while charges for cutting, handling, and hauling increased harvest expenses even more. Based on figures such as these, farmers believed

combines saved money. Moreover, the most optimistic champions of the combine contended that farmers only would use this implement during dry years while they returned to the binder in wet years. By so doing, they would be able to adjust their technological capabilities to the caprices of nature and, if not master it, respond to its dictates in a manner which gave them a competitive edge.[13]

In addition to the savings in labor costs and grain, combines sped the harvest. While binders averaged approximately 15 to 20 acres harvested per day and headers 20 to 30 acres, a 15-foot combine harvested 35 to 40 acres per day, or between 500 and 700 acres during a 14-day cutting season. Speed such as this reduced the risk from bad weather at harvest time and encouraged farmers to expand their production. Based on a harvest of 20 bushels per acre and $1 per bushel for wheat, a farmer with a 15-foot combine could earn an additional $6,920 by using this implement at maximum capacity. Even after the deduction of harvest expenses, most Great Plains farmers believed the adoption of the combine meant more money in the bank and the opportunity to increase the scale of their grain operations. By 1929, Great Plains farmers harvested an estimated 75 percent of their winter wheat with combines. Although no one knew how many combines farmers used at that time, in Kansas alone, estimates ranged from 16,000 to more than 20,000 of these implements.[14]

Swathers

In the spring wheat area of the northern Great Plains, farmers preferred the binder over the combine, because spring wheat did not ripen evenly, and it frequently contained many weeds. Both factors prevented the efficient harvest of dry wheat. In 1928 South Dakota farmers began using a special implement, called a swather, to cut the grain and put it in a windrow or swath about three feet wide. After several days of curing in the windrow, the grain and green weeds dried sufficiently to thresh properly. Then, the combine lifted the swath with a windrow pickup attachment that hooked to the front of the implement. The swather or windrower enabled a farmer to cut

By the mid-1930s, the power takeoff was a standard feature on tractors and combines. Here, it is clearly visible above the tongue or hook-up bar. The tabular auger system elevated the grain from the tank into a truck that pulled alongside. (Courtesy of the Kansas State Historical Society)

50 of the 63

Anti-friction Bearings used on this Gleaner Baldwin Combine are HYATT ROLLER BEARINGS

GOOD bearings make good equipment ... both of which are necessary to profitable farming. The well known Gleaner Baldwin Combines depend on Hyatt Roller Bearings in practically all bearing positions for efficient and carefree operation. These bearings require no attention other than an occasional lubrication; are enclosed in simple dustproof housings and keep moving parts in proper alignment for quiet and long lasting service.

HYATT
ROLLER BEARINGS
PRODUCT OF GENERAL MOTORS

This is the Mark of Hyatt Protection ... a red symbol with a gold border ... used by many builders of Hyattized equipment. It is a buyer's guide of permanent bearing satisfaction.

Hyatt Roller Bearings are preferred for all modern farm equipment. Their construction enables them to absorb the shocks of hard tasks. They are self-lubricating and self-cleaning. Hyatt equipped farm machines will not heat at bearing points. They will perform quietly and efficiently because loads are distributed over the length of the roller eliminating wear, and preventing looseness in bearing and other working parts.

HYATT ROLLER BEARING COMPANY
Newark   Detroit   Chicago   Pittsburgh   Oakland

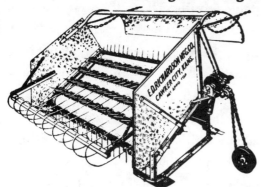

FLEXIBLE COMBINE PICK-UP
Light Weight   Runs Easy

Fits any Combine Harvester, Thresher, or common header, or Windrower.

Windshield at each end.

Either shoe can swing 16 inches up and down to fit uneven ground.

Lifts windrows as it goes.

Throws grain back on platform loose and ready to thresh.

Each shoe floats on the ground, weight being carried by spring in hold back chains.

Guaranteed to please or your money refunded.

Takes care of itself— You can get on tractor and drive.

Fingers cannot wear out at coils.

One man can attach or take off pickup.

See your dealer or write us for a real combine pick-up attachment. Slats, canvas and 200 fingers get all the grain. Will not pick up stones. Easy to attach; hinges to platform; flexible; fits uneven ground. Guaranteed to satisfy. Fine for wheat, oats, barley, flax, hersey, seed alfalfa, beans.

Made in Three Widths
60 In.	Wt. 275;	List	$105.00
68 In.	Wt. 295;	List	$112.50
84 In.	Wt. 330;	List	$125.00

F. O. B. Cawker City, Kans.

Dealers and Farmers Write for Catalog.

E. D. RICHARDSON MFG. CO., Cawker City, Kansas

In the Dakotas, grain farmers windrowed their crop with a swather. The grain dried sufficiently in several days to enable pickup with a combine. These John Deere windrowers worked on a North Dakota wheat field in 1930. Some farm implement companies, such as the E. D. Richardson Manufacturing Company in Cawker City, Kansas, built special attachments to improve the combine's pickup of the windrow. (Courtesy of the Deere & Company Archives)

his wheat as much as a week earlier than he could with a combine alone. When the wheat fully ripened, a farmer could cut with the combine for about 14 days; then he could work another week by using the pickup attachment for the previously swathed wheat. This technique reduced shattering and enabled a farmer to extend his harvest and expand his grain production.[15]

The windrowing method, however, had several disadvantages. High winds could scatter the swath, the windrowed grain was more susceptible to hail damage than shocked grain, and the pickup attachments on the combines often failed to collect all of the grain. Also, some-times pickup attachments did not deliver the straw continuously onto the combine's canvas conveyor belt to ensure the uniform flow of the grain to the threshing cylinder. Or it delivered too much grain thereby jamming the machine or stalling the engine. Nevertheless, windrowing made the combine profitable in the northern Great Plains. Farmers preferred the windrowing method because they were reluctant to delay their harvest for a week or more once the grain was ripe enough to cut with a binder.[16]

Self-Propelled Combines

During the mid-1940s, the self-propelled combine her-

Customs cutters began the wheat harvest in Texas and ended their trek northward in the Dakotas during the late autumn. Although they harvested winter wheat first, they often concluded with sunflowers after nearly six months on the road. (Courtesy of the Kansas State Historical Society)

alded the future for grain harvesters. By eliminating the tractor to pull the combine and the auxiliary engine or the power takeoff system to operate the machine, farmers streamlined their harvesting operations even more. By removing the tractor from the harvest, farmers gained an implement for other work, such as the immediate plowing of the stubble field after the grain had been cut. The elimination of the tractor and auxiliary engines from the harvesting process also reduced fuel expenses, because the combine's engine only needed to be large enough to power the machine. Tractors used for pulling a combine usually had far more power than was necessary. As a result, tractors used more fuel than combine engines. Moreover, self-propelled combines decreased the man-power requirement for operating the implement. Now, one person could harvest the crop. A driver, who hauled the grain from the field to the bin or nearby elevator, was the only additional worker required. Because the family usually could furnish the driver, there was no expense if that worker did not receive a wage.[17]

Self-propelled combines also eliminated grain losses when a farmer opened his grain field, that is, when the combine made its first round. Because tractor-pulled combines ordinarily had cutting tables to the right side of the implement, the tractor knocked down much of the grain in its path when the farmer made his first round in the field. The self-propelled combine also had greater maneuverability, enabling a farmer to swing around areas of unripened grain with relative ease in order to come back at a later time. In addition, self-propelled combines had less difficulty passing down narrow country roads because the cutter bar was centered in front of the implement, not off to the side.[18]

The self-propelled combines operated with greater efficiency than the larger tractor-drawn models. A seven-foot, self-propelled combine, for example, operating at five miles per hour could do as much as a 12-foot, tractor-drawn implement with an auxiliary engine, and it cost about the same as a six-foot combine with an auxiliary engine. Some farm machinery experts, however, feared

Implement manufacturers began building self-propelled combines during the 1940s. With this implement one man could harvest and thresh the wheat crop. Still, the wheat harvest remained hot, tiresome work. At first, custom cutters considered anyone who used an umbrella for shade to be a "sissy." (Courtesy of the Kansas State Historical Society)

56

the self-propelled combine might lend itself so readily to custom cutting that the market would decline precipitously, all to the detriment of the farm implement industry. During the mid-1940s, however, ownership of a combine for those farmers who could afford one provided the independence that they so enjoyed. With their own combine, they did not have to endure the agony of waiting for the custom cutter to arrive while worrying whether their already dead-ripe wheat would be lost to a hail-storm or shatter from the heads in the wind.[19]

Wheat farmers in the Great Plains certainly did not worry about the farm implement companies driving them-

selves out of business through technological change, nor did company officials. In the war year of 1944, for example, Massey-Harris, a Canadian firm, sold 500 of its 14-foot, self-propelled models for cash to an equal number of farm operators, known as the Massey-Harris Harvest Brigade, on the Great Plains. Each operator pledged to cut 2,000 acres by following the harvest northward from their points of origin in Texas, Oklahoma, and Kansas. Massey-Harris wanted to showcase its new implement, and company officials hoped their machine would cut one million acres of wheat and save 300,000 man-hours over tractor-drawn models, regardless of size, for an estimated savings

Self-propelled combines virtually replaced tractor-drawn implements during the 1960s. Although the combine required only one operator, some one, often the farmer's wife, drove the truck from the field to the grain elevator. Because farmers usually did not pay themselves or family members a wage, they could absorb this labor cost. As a result, the combine became even more cost efficient. In 1947, the John Deere 55 combine was the company's first self-propelled combine. (Courtesy of the Deere & Company Archives)

Hillside combines enabled farmers to raise small grains on moderately rolling land. The cutter bar and platform pivoted to match the slope of the land while hydraulic cylinders kept the body level. The wheels were synchronized so that one lowered at the same degree the other raised. Automatic leveling became a standard feature on hillside combines after 1955. John Deere introduced the 55-H Hillside Combine in 1954, it played an instrumental role in revolutionizing the wheat harvest in the Pacific Northwest. (Courtesy of the Deere & Company Archives)

International Harvester introduced its Axial-Flow combines in 1977. A nine-foot axial rotor, aligned lengthwise, tumbled the crop rearward across rasps, concaves, and grates. With the threshing cylinder turned lengthwise to the combine, high centrifugal force can be used to separate the grain and straw, and greater threshing capacity can be achieved compared to other cylinder alignments. Agricultural engineers spent more than one million man-hours perfecting this design. (Courtesy of the Smithsonian Institution)

This IHC combine harvested rice near Stuttgart, Arkansas, in August 1982. The pickup reel had wire fingers that gathered the crop and fed it to the cutter bar. Prior to World War II, combines used for harvesting rice had steel crawler tracks for traction. After the war, rubber tires became affordable and more convenient for moving combines down country roads. (Courtesy of the Smithsonian Institution)

of 60 percent in labor alone. Company officials also anticipated that their machines would save 750,000 bushels of wheat that otherwise would be lost by tractor-drawn models. Whether Massey-Harris achieved these goals is moot. Most important, this farm implement company and a host of farmers had high expectations for the self-propelled combine, and each profited from the needs of the other, as well as being patriotic.[20]

Still, change comes slowly. Relatively high costs and previous investment in tractor-drawn models retarded the wide-scale adoption of the self-propelled combine. The engineers at the farm implement companies had to design a self-propelled combine that was simple to operate, repair, and control as well as one that would harvest under a wide variety of climatic and topographical conditions. The self-propelled combine also had to have proper balance, light weight, great carrying capacity, and adequate power for cutting, threshing, and propulsion. Although

most wheat farmers used combines to harvest their crop by the end of World War II, tractor-drawn models still predominated until 1960.[21]

Soybean and Rice Harvesting

Agricultural engineers and farmers also applied the combine to harvesting problems other than those found among wheat farmers in the Great Plains and Midwest. Soybeans, for example, easily shattered from the pod during the harvest as farmers used mowers, binders, windrowers, and threshing machines to bring in the crop. During the mid-1920s, combine tests in Illinois reduced seed losses to about 9 percent, but this was the best result that could be achieved for the next half-century. Part of the problem resulted from rigid cutter bars which could not follow the contours of the ground and cut the vines at the proper level. By 1930, floating cutter bars clipped the vines close to the soil, but a satisfactory pickup reel still had not been developed to lift the vines over the sickle and onto the canvas apron which led to the threshing cylinder. During the early 1930s, however, the Hume-Love Company in Garfield, Washington, developed a pickup reel that used steel tines instead of wooden slats. As the combine moved forward, a linkage and cam kept the tines rotating. The tines caught the vines and lifted them gently over the cutter bar. Still, harvest losses were not improved until the 1970s, when Deere & Company developed a row-crop header that attached to a combine. This header used a rotary knife to sever the plants on each row and an auger to convey the vines to a threshing cylinder. This innovation reduced harvesting losses to about 4 percent of the crop. In 1977, the White Company introduced a flexible, knife-like cutter bar, set at a slight pitch, which sliced through the vines better than any other device. This innovation reduced seed losses to about 1 percent, thereby increasing profits.[22]

During the 1930s, agricultural engineers also mounted combines on a track-type chassis for rice harvesting. Although steel crawler tracks provided adequate traction in the rice fields, sandy soil caused excessive wear and the tracks damaged roads when the combines moved from field to field. Rubber tracks provided a viable alternative, but this technology remained prohibitively expensive still in the late 1940s. Agricultural engineers also developed a special threshing mechanism for flax so the seed and straw

Although agricultural engineers experimented with the combine for the soybean harvest during the 1920s, this crop could not be successfully machine harvested until the 1970s. At that time, agricultural engineers at the Deere and White companies developed a new cutting system that severed the vines without causing the beans to shatter from the pods. (Courtesy of the University of Missouri Agricultural Extension, photo by Duane Dailey)

would exit from the machine undamaged and ready for processing into oil and paper.[23]

In 1939, Deere & Company introduced the Model 12A combine. This combine was well suited for small acreages. It operated off the tractor's power takeoff (PTO), and it featured a left-hand cut. The 12A became Deere's most popular PTO combine. By 1952, when production ceased, more than 116,000 units had been built. (Courtesy of the Deere & Company Archives)

In 1954, Deere offered the first corn head attachment for a combine. This attachment harvested two rows with endless chain feeders. Corn harvesting required combines to have more power and stronger construction than the machines that harvested small grains. (Courtesy of the Deere & Company Archives)

Corn Combines

In addition to these developments, as early as 1928, agricultural engineers also experimented with combines for harvesting corn. This crop, however, did not lend itself to mechanical harvesting as readily as small grains. By the late 1920s, the combine left approximately 50 percent of the corn crop in the field. The corn stalks easily choked the combine and limited the harvest to no more than two rows at once at a snail's pace of one mile per hour. These problems required agricultural engineers to devise satisfactory gathering and feeding devices.[24]

In 1929, the Gleaner-Baldwin Harvester Company built the first successful corn combine, which it offered for sale the following year. This machine used four circular saws, working in pairs, behind four gathering chains. This two-row implement cut the stalks and deposited the corn on an auger conveyor which delivered it to the threshing cylinder. Estimates of grain loss in the field ranged from 2 to 15 percent. The Baldwin combine sold for $1,675 while the combination wheat and corn machine marketed at $2,025. This latter conversion could be made only with some difficulty by changing the threshing cylinder and the cutting, conveying, and feeding mechanisms. A Model A Ford industrial engine powered the Gleaner-Baldwin corn combine while a 15- to 30-horsepower tractor could pull the implement without difficulty.[25]

The Gleaner-Baldwin machine became the first successful implement to combine corn, but the company soon foundered in the economic quagmire of the Great Depression. Even so, the ultimate wide-scale adoption of the corn combine did not depend on solving technical problems such as cutting and threshing tough, large plants, but on the development of efficient grain dryers for the harvested crop. Corn that had been harvested with a combine usually had a moisture content high enough to lower the market price, and it spoiled in the bin. To be stored safely corn should not have a moisture content over 14 percent. Shelled corn, however, dried in about three days compared to ear corn which took about ten days.[26]

While the Great Depression and World War II prevented major expansion or the perfection of new innovations, such as the corn combine, farmers continued to cut their crop by hand or to use the corn picker which snapped the ears from the stalks and husked them. By the early 1950s, however, agricultural engineers had developed a combine that could cut and thresh corn efficiently with a moisture content as high as 26 percent. This mechanical ability meant that farmers could begin their harvest sooner than when they used a picker. The higher moisture content prevented the loss of kernels during the cutting, snapping, and delivery of the ears to the threshing cylinder, whereas the picker required dryer corn to work efficiently. Affordable and efficient grain dryers now enabled farmers to store damp, combine-harvested corn.[27]

In 1954, Deere & Company became the first farm implement company to provide a corn head that was adaptable to a combine. The Deere corn head collected two rows at once with endless chain feeders, and it had an auger system similar to the earlier Gleaner-Baldwin, but a different cutting mechanism to avoid patent infringement. Soon thereafter, the corn head became a standard attachment for all combines, but it required as much as five times more power than combines designed to harvest small grains. Corn combines, such as these, also had to have a stronger grain bin and chassis than combines designed for wheat, barley, and oats, because damp corn substantially increased the weight and strain on the machine.[28]

In 1975, Sperry New Holland introduced a new combine, the TR Twin Rotor, to improve the corn harvest. This machine had greater threshing capacity because it used centrifugal separation with the threshing cylinder's axis running parallel to the combine's advance. These axial flow combines, however, tended to break the straw which hampered later baling. Axial combines also required more power under damp-straw conditions. Even so, these machines provided greater harvesting efficiency, easier operation, and repair.[29]

Conclusion

In retrospect, farmers on the Great Plains had many advantages that enabled them to adopt the combine before that machine became technically feasible for farmers in the sub-humid Midwest and the humid South. On the Great Plains the level terrain and the absence of obstructions, such as stumps or rocks in the fields, permitted combines to operate without the danger of upsetting or damage. The hard winter wheat varieties also ripened uniformly to permit harvest of the entire crop at one time and thereby avoid the mixture of damp, green wheat with dry wheat in the bin. Moreover, the fields of the Great Plains generally were not troubled with weeds that increased the moisture of the grain in the combine's cylinder.[30]

In general, combines enabled farmers to make considerable savings by reducing their hired labor costs. Combines eliminated the need for harvest workers to handle the grain three times by shocking it, by pitching it onto a wagon for transport to the stack, and by pitching it again into the threshing machine. Combines cut the grain, threshed it, and delivered the grain by auger to wagon or truck. Combines also helped change the nature of the labor force in the Great Plains. Before the wide-scale adoption of these implements during the 1920s, many itinerant workers came into the wheat belt of the Great Plains during harvest and threshing time. Combines, however, eliminated the need for these workers. After the adoption of the combine, harvest labor primarily came from the permanent residents of the region. High school and college men from the nearby small towns filled many positions on neighborhood farms until completion of the harvest. Moreover, the wheat harvest now required, instead of an adequate number of brawny itinerant workers, semi-skilled tractor drivers, combine operators, and truck drivers.[31]

Combines also fostered other technological adjustments among wheat farmers. Prior to the mid-1920s, for example, many farmers had used the lister plow to prepare the seed bed. The lister plow, however, left the fields with steep ridges and rough furrows. Farmers quickly found they had to follow these ridges with their tractors and combines because crossing the furrows not only produced a rough ride but also prevented the uniform cutting of the grain stalks. As a result, farmers increasingly used the one-way disk plow that turned the soil, buried the trash and left the surface relatively smooth for planting and harvesting. Moreover, combines reduced the number of horses used at harvest time and, as the number of horses declined, farmers seeded acreage previously planted in hay or forage crops with higher paying cash crops for human food.[32]

The combine not only helped increase the expansion of the wheat acreage but also the size of farms — in part to enable the most efficient use of these large implements. Certainly, the adoption of the combine helped the most financially sound and efficient farmers to increase their profits and to buy out neighbors who were less successful. Some farmers, however, feared that combines would eliminate the need for the family farmer and that corporate agriculture soon would bring complete industrialization to the farm. Although this fear was never realized, combines

During the 1980s, combines had air-conditioned cabs and headlights as standard features. These conveniences enabled farmers to harvest their wheat crop comfortably and, if humidity remained low, at night. In 1984, this John Deere 7720 Titan II harvested wheat in Oklahoma. (Courtesy of the Deere & Company Archives)

did contribute to the demise of diversified farming on the Great Plains. At the same time, the smaller combine models probably enabled wheat farmers in the older portions of the wheat-growing region, such as the Old Northwest, to maintain production. Although wheat prices remained low during the 1920s and 1930s, the reduction in harvesting costs, which the combine made possible, enabled farmers in that region to earn some profit from small grain crops even though they were no longer competitive with wheat farmers in the Great Plains.[33]

Even so, in order to use the combine most efficiently, farmers frequently expanded their acreage by renting or purchasing more land. Greater dependence on wheat, however, increasingly placed these farmers at the mercy of nature and market prices beyond their control. Moreover, the combine, together with the gasoline tractor, helped farmers expand wheat production into the submarginal regions of the Great Plains. This dry region, largely composed of wind-deposited soil, however, could support the cultivation of wheat only during seasons of above-normal precipitation or when the price of wheat merited the risk. Much of this region should have been left in the protective hold of the native grasses, because when drought occurred, as it did during the 1930s, the exposed soil drifted with the wind. The result was the creation of the Dust Bowl and a wind-erosion menace that remained until normal precipitation returned nearly a decade later and until the federal government implemented a massive soil conservation program.[34]

The wide-scale adoption of the combine helped cause other far-reaching problems in the countryside. By speeding the harvest, local elevators now had to handle the bulk of the crop within a few weeks' time. Elevator operators no longer had the luxury of a time lag of several weeks or months between harvest and receipt of the threshed grain. Frequently, their equipment and facilities were inadequate to handle the job. Like the tractor and other powered implements, combines also contributed to the long-running decline of rural population, because this technology enabled the most successful farmers to expand their holdings by purchasing the land of those less fortunate. With fewer farmers on the land, rural schools and churches often no longer had sufficient pupils or members to merit operation. A drop in the rural population also adversely affected the prosperity of local merchants.[35]

At the same time, however, the combine helped local merchants, because farmers could immediately sell their grain for cash which they then could apply to outstanding bills. Moreover, farmers no longer needed credit to help meet their operating and household expenses between harvest and threshing time. Combines also boosted the financial fortunes of local implement dealers and stimulated the purchase of tractors and trucks to help work more acres and to haul more wheat to the elevator. Indeed, with the adoption of the combine, a farmer easily might invest between $50,000 and $100,000 in his agricultural enterprise, if he also owned the land and other equipment

during the 1920s. This heavy investment, however, was more than most farmers could accumulate in a lifetime. Large investments in machinery, such as combines, boded ill for those farmers who could not adequately manage their operations in order to meet their mortgages and bills from installment purchases.[36]

Combines also encouraged one-crop specialized agriculture, and farmers had to become better businessmen to manage their affairs. They also contributed to the problem of surplus production of wheat which, in turn, kept prices low and taxed the ability of the railroads to move the grain to market in a timely fashion. In addition, farmers had to learn to adjust the traditional manner in which they began the wheat harvest when they used combines. With the binder, for example, the wheat crop had to be cut while the grain remained damp to prevent it from shattering when cut, shocked, and hauled to the threshing machine. After several days, the sheaves had dried sufficiently to thresh properly, and the wheat could be stored without danger of spoilage or heating. In contrast, farmers had to combine their wheat crop when it was dead ripe. If cut at the proper time, wheat threshed and stored well. Many new combine owners, however, tended to cut their wheat too soon and suffered lower prices from selling damp grain as a result. In addition, combines could harvest and thresh damp grain without difficulty, so farmers had to learn by the touch, the smell, and the bite of the grain when the wheat crop was ready for harvesting. They also had to learn when to begin with their machines in the morning after the dew dried off and when to shut them off at night before the moisture content of the grain increased from cool, damp air or the onset of dew. Several seasons usually were required before they became skilled practitioners of this new harvesting method. Farmers who harvested with combines also took greater risks with the weather, because binders enabled them to begin their harvest several days before they could with a combine. While wheat farmers waited for their grain to ripen, they were at the mercy of bad weather — heavy rain, wind, and hail — all common products of a summertime thunderstorm on the Great Plains.[37]

Combines had other affects as well. Like threshing machines of the late nineteenth century, the twentieth-century combine lightened the work of the wheat farmer's wife. With fewer hands needed at harvest time, her cooking responsibilities lessened considerably, but she might become the truck driver. For her, the combine made life easier in the summertime. Farmers also had to keep their fields clear of rocks and other obstructions as well as prepare a smoothly plowed field for planting and harvesting. They also had to select varieties of grain that did not lodge in the combine or shatter from the heads. Before the advent of self-propelled combines, farmers had to purchase tractors to pull these machines. As a result, combines indirectly contributed to the further mechanization of the farm and directly to the social and economic status of the owner. By 1950, the combine had mechanized the wheat harvest from the Canadian border to Texas. Today, the combine remains a symbol of capital-intensive, technological change in the Great Plains and Far West.[38]

NOTES

1. R. Douglas Hurt, *American Farm Tools: From Hand-Power to Steam-Power* (Manhattan, KS: Sunflower University Press, 1982): 77-79.
2. *Ibid.*, 79.
3. *Ibid.*
4. *Ibid.*, 75-80; Thomas D. Isern, *Custom Combining on the Great Plains: A History* (Norman: University of Oklahoma Press, 1981), 13, 15; W. E. Grimes, R. S. Kifer, and J. A. Hodges, "The Effect of the Combined Harvester-Thresher on Farm Organization in Southwestern Kansas and Northwestern Oklahoma," Kansas Agricultural Experiment Station, *Circular 142* (1928), 7; L. A. Reynoldson, "The Combined Harvester-Thresher in the Great Plains," United States Department of Agriculture, *Technical Bulletin 70* (1928), 3; Gabriel Lundy, K. H. Klages, and J. F. Goss, "The Use of the Combine in South Dakota," South Dakota Agricultural Experiment Station, *Bulletin 244* (1929), 4-5; R. C. Miller and Alva H. Benton, "Combine Harvesting in North Dakota," North Dakota Agricultural Experiment Station, *Bulletin 220* (1928), 115; J. O. Ellsworth and R. W. Baird, "The Combine Harvester on Oklahoma Farms, 1926," Oklahoma Agricultural Experiment Station, *Bulletin 162* (1927), 3; H. P. Smith and Robert Spillman, "Harvesting Grain With the Combined-Harvester Thresher in Northwest Texas," Texas Agricultural Experiment Station, *Bulletin 373* (1927), 7; A. E. Starch and R. M. Merrill, "The Combined Harvester-Thresher in Montana," Montana Agricultural Experiment Station, *Bulletin 230* (1930), 6-7.
5. Reynoldson, "The Combined Harvester-Thresher in the Great Plains," 3-4; Lundy, Klages, and Goss, "The Use of the Combine in South Dakota, 57; Grimes, Kifer, and Hodges, "The Effect of the Combined Harvester-Thresher on Farm Organization in Southwestern Kansas and Northwestern Oklahoma," 7.
6. Reynoldson, "The Combined Harvester-Thresher in the Great Plains," 9-10.
7. *Ibid.*, 13-15.
8. Don D. Lescohier, "Sources of Supply and Conditions of Employment of Harvest Labor in the Wheat Belt," United States Department of Agriculture, *Bulletin 1211* (1924), 1, 16, 29; Don D. Lescohier, "Harvest Labor Problems in the Wheat Belt," United States Department of Agriculture, *Bulletin 1020* (1922), 1; Don D. Lescohier, "Conditions Affecting the Demand for Harvest Labor in the Wheat Belt," United States Department of Agriculture, *Bulletin 1230*, (1924), 19.
9. Reynoldson, "The Combined Harvester-Thresher in the Great Plains," 21-23, 33.
10. Ellsworth and Baird, "The Combine Harvester on Oklahoma Farms," 10; Reynoldson, "The Combined Harvester-Thresher in the Great Plains," 33.
11. Reynoldson, "The Combined Harvester-Thresher in the Great Plains," 37.
12. Ellsworth and Baird, "The Combine Harvester on Oklahoma Farms," 6, 8-9; Starch and Merrill, "The Combined Harvester-Thresher in Montana," 14, 58; Grimes, Kifer, and Hodges, "The Effect of the Combined Harvester-Thresher on Farm Organization in Southwestern Kansas and Northwestern Oklahoma," 11; Reynoldson, "The Combined Harvester-Thresher in the Great Plains," 40, 43; Lundy, Klages, and Goss, "The Use of the Combine in South Dakota," 52.
13. W. F. MacGregor, "The Combined Harvester-Thresher," *Agricultural Engineering*, 6 (May 1925): 103.
14. *Ibid.*; Lescohier, "Conditions Affecting the Demand for Harvest Labor in the Wheat Belt," 17-18; Reynoldson, "The Combined Harvester-Thresher in the Great Plains," 51-52; Grimes, Kifer, and Hodges, "The Effect of the Combined Harvester-Thresher on Farm Organization in Southwestern Kansas and Northwestern Oklahoma," 10; W. E. Grimes, "The Effect of the Combined Harvester-Thresher on Farming in a Wheat-Growing Region," *Scientific Agriculture*, 9 (Aug. 1929): 773.
15. Isern, *Custom Combining on the Great Plains*, 17; Grimes, "The Effect of the Combined Harvester-Thresher on Farming in a Wheat-Growing Region," 775; D. E. Wient and R. L. Patty, "Combining Grain in Weed-Free Fields," South Dakota Agricultural Experiment Station, *Bulletin 251* (1930); Lundy, Kifer, and Goss, "The Use of the Combine in South Dakota," 56; Starch and Merrill, "The Combined Harvester-Thresher in Montana," 32-33, 35.
16. Starch and Merrill, "The Combined Harvester-Thresher in Montana," 30; E. A. Hardy, "The Combine in the Prairie Provinces," *Agricultural Engineering*, 10 (Feb. 1929): 55-56; Hiram M. Drache, *Beyond the Furrow: Some Keys to Successful Farming in the Twentieth Century* (Danville, IL: Interstate Printers, 1976), 117.
17. Joe Tucker, "The Self-Propelled Combine," *Agricultural Engineering*, 25 (Sept. 1944): 333-335.
18. *Ibid.*, 336.
19. *Ibid.*, 333-334.
20. *Ibid.*, 334-335.
21. Tom Carroll, "Basic Requirements in the Design and Development of the Self-Propelled Combine," *Agricultural Engineering*, 29 (Mar. 1948): 101; John T. Schlebecker, *Whereby We Thrive: A History of American Farming, 1607-1972* (Ames: Iowa State University Press), 297.
22. Graeme Quick and Wesley Buchele, *The Grain Harvesters* (St. Joseph, MI: American Society of Agricultural Engineers, 1978), 225-232.
23. Carroll, "Basic Requirements in the Design and Development of the Self-Propelled Combine," 103.
24. E. G. McKibbin, "Harvesting Corn With a Combine," *Agricultural Engineering*, 10 (July 1929): 231-232.
25. C. A. Logan, "The Development of a Corn Combine," *Agricultural Engineering*, 12 (July 1931): 277-278.
26. *Ibid.*, 278; Quick and Buchele, *The Grain Harvesters*, 219.
27. Quick and Buchele, *The Grain Harvesters*, 220-221; L. W. Hurlbut, "More Efficient Corn Harvesting," *Agricultural Engineering*, 36 (Dec. 1955): 791-792; Schlebecker, *Whereby We Thrive*, 297.
28. Quick and Buchele, *The Grain Harvesters*, 221-222.
29. *Ibid.*, 245-246, 256; Roy Bainer, "Science and Technology in Western Agriculture," *Agricultural History*, 49 (Jan. 1975): 58-60, 67-68; Schlebecker, *Whereby We Thrive*, 252.
30. Grimes, "The Effect of the Combined Harvester-Thresher on Farming in a Wheat-Growing Region," 773.
31. *Ibid.*, 774; MacGregor, "The Combined Harvester-Thresher," 102.
32. Grimes, "The Effect of the Combined Harvester-Thresher on Farming in a Wheat-Growing Region," 775; MacGregor, "The Combined Harvester-Thresher," 102.
33. Grimes, "The Effect of the Combined Harvester-Thresher on Farm Organization in Southwestern Kansas and Northwestern Oklahoma," 27-28.
34. *Ibid.*, 8, 228; R. Douglas Hurt, *The Dust Bowl: An Agricultural and Social History* (Chicago: Nelson-Hall, Publishers, 1981).
35. Grimes, "The Effect of the Combined Harvester-Thresher on Farming in a Wheat-Growing Region," 777-779; Grimes, "The Effect of the Combined Harvester-Thresher on Farm Organization in Southwestern Kansas and Northwestern Oklahoma," 9.
36. Grimes, "The Effect of the Combined Harvester-Thresher on Farming in a Wheat-Growing Region," 779, 781; Isern, *Custom Combining on the Great Plains*, 20.
37. L. C. Aicher, "Problems of the Combine Harvester," *Report of the Kansas Board of Agriculture for the Quarter Ending March, 1930*, 101-103; Lundy, Klages, and Goss, "The Use of the Combine in South Dakota," 5-6, 54; Starch and Merrill, "The Combined Harvester-Thresher in Montana," 45.
38. Thomas D. Isern, *Bull Threshers and Bindlestiffs: Harvesting & Threshing on the North American Plains* (Lawrence: University Press of Kansas, 1990).

Chapter 4

Irrigation in the West

IRRIGATION is an ancient agricultural practice long associated with intensive human labor and, until the twentieth century, it was largely restricted to areas near streams and reservoirs. More than 4,000 years ago the Egyptians and the Chinese used irrigation to increase agricultural productivity. In the Western Hemisphere early Indian civilizations built irrigation canals in the Southwest. In present-day Arizona, for example, the Hohokam developed an extensive canal system as early as A.D. 800 that rivaled the Old World farmers along the Euphrates and Tigris Rivers. On the central Plains, Indians, who farmed along Beaver Creek in present-day Kansas about 1650, also supplemented annual rainfall with irrigation. As late as the turn of the twentieth century, however, farmers and scientists alike considered the Great Plains, particularly the High Plains, nonirrigable.[1]

During the early twentieth century, some Great Plains farmers used windmills for irrigation. In order to do so, even on a moderate scale, they had to build a reservoir. This impoundment held the water pumped from the ground and ensured a consistent flow to the field. Windmills, however, were sufficient only for irrigating vegetable gardens and fruit trees, because this technology could not pump a great volume of water. At best a windmill only irrigated several acres, and it did not support large-scale irrigation on the Great Plains. The high cost of maintenance for windmills also prevented widespread use for irrigation, particularly if a farmer could afford a comparable investment for a pump powered by a gas or steam engine. Most windmill irrigation occurred during the early twentieth century in southern Kansas and north-central California.[2]

Pump Irrigation

On the Great Plains irrigation worked best when pumps lifted the water from beneath the surface and provided a consistent flow to the fields. By the late nineteenth and early twentieth centuries Western farmers began using centrifugal pumps. These pumps delivered several hundred gallons of water per minute, and this technology enabled farmers to tap ground water supplies with shallow wells, particularly in the river valleys. Electric motors and gas and steam engines powered these pumps. Because each irrigation pump could cost almost $400, while the well and engine or power plant were additional expenses, few farmers could afford the investment. Moreover, the

During the early twentieth century, some Western farmers tried to expand production by using windmills to pump water for irrigation. Because of limited pumping capacity, these efforts were restricted to small-scale endeavors. In July 1925, this wooden-towered windmill filled the stock tank and irrigated a garden for this family in Chase County, Nebraska. (Courtesy of the Nebraska State Historical Society)

increased profits from irrigated crops often did not justify this financial commitment. The Western farmer's general lack of experience with irrigation methods and gasoline engines also slowed expansion of pump irrigation.[3]

After 1930, technological change in the form of powerful turbine pumps, movable sprinklers, and gated pipe enabled farmers to irrigate large tracts of land far removed from traditional water sources. These improvements not only permitted farmers to pump more water from great depths, but the new technology also became increasingly affordable. By the 1930s, a farmer in West Texas, for example, needed little more than $2,000 for a well, casing, pump, and engine to mine water from nearly 200 feet beneath the surface. If a farmer built his well house from lumber already at hand and used an engine from a junked automobile, the investment decreased considerably. Moreover, the federal government provided modest help under the Water Facilities Act of 1937 and through the Federal Housing Administration to help farmers develop pump irrigation. Local banks, irrigation equipment companies, and pump dealers also provided financial support. With increased reliance on irrigation, farmers in the southern Plains changed their cropping patterns from wheat to cotton, grain sorghum, and alfalfa. In the central Plains, they planted corn, and in both areas they began to use irrigation to ensure maximum production instead of merely for crop insurance. By so doing, irrigation changed the looks of the land.[4]

Irrigation Methods

During the 1930s, the North Platte River provided nearly all of the irrigation water in Nebraska. Most of the farmers who drew upon this source used the technique known as flooding, commonly called "wild flooding," to irrigate their crops. This method involved opening the bank of an irrigation ditch to let a thin sheet of water spread across a field. Flooding required reasonably level land so the entire surface could be covered with the water. For land

Windmill irrigation systems were known as "pumping plants." Because of low pumping capacity a reservoir was needed to ensure an appropriate flow to the fields. This Gem windmill and reservoir enabled the irrigation of nearby fields in Finney County, Kansas. (Courtesy of the Kansas State Historical Society)

Irrigation agriculture is not confined to the American West. This irrigation pumping plant and canal furnished water to nearby Louisiana rice fields in January 1906. (Courtesy of the Smithsonian Institution)

After 1910, steam and internal combustion engines and electric motors enabled farmers to use large capacity pumps. These power sources and pumps continuously delivered a great volume of water and thereby eliminated the need for a windmill and reservoir. (Courtesy of the Kansas State Historical Society)

that had a rough surface or a considerable slope, contour ditches worked best. These small irrigation ditches carried the water to the fields on a contoured grade. By blocking or checking the water at various locations, it would overflow the ditch and spread across the field. These ditches were spaced 60 to 200 feet apart, and a farmer could make them easily with a moldboard plow. Because flooding eroded the soil, farmers primarily used this technique on closely growing crops, such as alfalfa, sweet clover, and small grains. The flooding method worked most efficiently to get water into the soil quickly, while land that had an irregular surface or a considerable slope could be irrigated by the contour ditch method.[5]

By the mid-1950s, Great Plains farmers primarily used the furrow rather than the flooding technique. This irrigation method utilized a gated pipe or ditch that ran along the upper edge of a field. Deep furrows that ran at right angles or on the contour to the pipe or head ditch carried the water between the plants. Siphon tubes sucked the water from the head ditch into the furrows. If a farmer used gated pipe instead of a ditch, the holes or gates in the pipe enable the water to pour into the furrows. The intake rate of the soil, the amount of water applied, and the slope of the land determined the length of the furrows and the size of the irrigated field. Low absorption rates, for example, enabled furrows to stretch for a quarter mile or more across the land. This irrigation technique did not require the land to be perfectly level, because the water only traveled down the furrows. It did not spread uniformly across a field.

Although farmers sometimes had difficulty getting a consistent amount of water to flow in the furrows, the water penetrated the soil slowly, and it provided an excellent irrigation of the crop.[6]

Western farmers also used the border irrigation method. This technique resembled flooding. It involved laying the land out in strips that were level across but which sloped away at a 1-percent grade from the head ditch to the end of the field. This method required graded borders or dikes that ran down the outer edge of a field. Farmers used these dikes to confine the water to the field after it had been released from the head ditch. Level border irrigation resembled the graded border technique except that the field was level both across and from end to end, and it remained closed at the end to prevent the loss of water. Level border irrigation enabled the uniform flooding of a field, and it became a popular method in the Southwest, especially for alfalfa, small grains, and closely growing crops. This technique enabled quick application and uniform distribution of water.[7]

Sprinkler irrigation became popular in the Pacific Northwest about 1930. It involved spraying water over a field with a perforated pipe or nozzle. Dairy farmers in the Pacific Northwest found sprinkler irrigation beneficial to ensure pasture growth during the dry months of July and August. Instead of losing milk production during the summer, sprinkler irrigation enabled dairy farmers to maintain productivity and income. With their increased profits, dairy farmers could complete payments on their sprinkler system after one or two seasons — a significant achievement during the Great Depression.[8]

Farmers in Southern California also adopted sprinkler irrigation during the early 1930s. By 1932, more than 100 growers used sprinklers. They preferred sprinkler irrigation to furrow irrigation because they lost less water to evaporation as it moved to the fields in pipes. In addition, they could better control the amount of water applied to their fields. By the early 1950s, orchard growers throughout the West rapidly shifted from furrow to sprinkler irrigation, particularly along the Hood River of Oregon and in the Yakima and Okanogan Valleys of Washington. Sprinklers enabled orchard growers to irrigate their trees on steep lands while avoiding soil erosion and the waste of water.[9]

Sprinklers were advantageous for land so level that water would not run across it or down a furrow. Moreover, sprinklers were well suited for land too rough for surface irrigation or too shallow for leveling. And, farmers preferred sprinkler irrigation where the porous soil could not hold surface water, where inadequate stream flow prevented furrow or flooding methods, and where expensive water and labor prevailed. In addition, sprinklers enabled farmers to irrigate lands that otherwise would have remained in dryland agricultural crops or pasture. At first, however, high costs, inefficient design, and poor mobility restricted the acceptance of sprinkler systems. Some of these systems, for example, had to be moved by hand. This procedure involved considerable labor to uncouple, move, and recouple the irrigation pipe. Other systems could be moved by tractors, because the pipe and sprinklers were mounted on skids or wheels or were attached to a movable boom.[10]

Sprinkler irrigation became increasingly popular, and it spread rapidly. Portable pipe and couplings made it more viable than ever before, and many farmers began using sprinklers to irrigate crops on land not suitable for surface irrigation. In 1946, for example, sprinklers irrigated fewer than 250,000 acres in the United States, but by 1954 farmers irrigated an estimated three million acres with this

This pumping plant tapped the Ogallala aquifer near Garden City in Finney County, Kansas, sometime between 1910 and 1925. With the water table close to the surface, farmers, who could afford the investment, drilled a well and pumped the water into a ditch or wooden flume for travel to the fields. The steam traction engine behind the drilling rig powered the pump. (Courtesy of the Kansas State Historical Society)

Some farmers built a house to protect their well, pump, and power source. This well house sheltered an electric motor. Note the electric meter at the left side of the shed. By catching the water first in a cattle tank, these farmers slowed soil erosion and enabled greater control as they channeled it to the fields. (Courtesy of the Nebraska State Historical Society)

Few farmers on the High Plains of Kansas and Texas worried about the depletion of the ground water supply during the early twentieth century. By the late twentieth century, however, unrestricted pumping had jeopardized the future of pump irrigation. (Courtesy of the Kansas State Historical Society)

Irrigation enabled Great Plains farmers to raise crops other than dryland wheat, such as sugar beets. The pumping plant housed beneath the drilling tower (r.) supplied the water to this head ditch in Meade County, Kansas. (Courtesy of the Kansas State Historical Society)

method. With sprinkler irrigation expanding at an estimated rate of 500,000 acres annually by the mid-1950s, adequate water supply rather than suitable terrain and cost became the primary limiting factors for its adoption.[11]

The center-pivot sprinkler eliminated most irrigation labor problems. Invented by Frank Zybach of Columbus, Nebraska, while farming in eastern Colorado, patented in 1952, and marketed the following year, the system consisted of sprinklers mounted on a six-inch pipe supported by a row of movable towers. The water entered the pipe from the source at the center of the field and propelled the system in a continuous circle. The sprinklers applied increasing amounts of water away from the well to ensure a uniform application across the field as the system revolved. Because the pipe was at least eight feet above the ground, only the narrow wheels interfered with the growing crops. The center-pivot sprinkler also enabled the farmer to irrigate automatically, and it could apply fertilizer at the same time that it supplied water. Most center-pivot systems cover 133 acres of a 160-acre field every three or four days and apply one inch of water per revolution. Special adapters can be added to swing out and cover the corners of the quarter section in order to irrigate nearly the entire 160 acres. The largest systems irrigate a section, or 640 acres. These big center-pivot systems required one-half mile of eight-inch pipe and 20 towers to support the pipe and sprinklers.[12]

Center-pivot sprinklers changed irrigation from a labor-intensive to a labor-extensive agricultural practice because more acres could be irrigated with less work than ever before. On the Great Plains, however, farmers were slow to

Ditch irrigation required the farmer to block a head or lateral ditch and to open the banks to let the water flow down the furrows of the field. This farmer irrigated sugar beets with the furrow method near Scottsbluff, Nebraska. (Courtesy of the Nebraska State Historical Society)

adopt the center-pivot system because of cost. By the late 1960s, though, they had enough confidence in the center-pivot system to make the necessary investment, and sprinkler systems, primarily center-pivot, irrigated 400,000 acres by 1973 — nearly a four-fold increase since 1955.[13]

The Kansas Experience

Twentieth-century irrigation developments in the West can be exemplified by the experience of Kansas farmers on the Great Plains. Modern irrigation in the Kansas Plains

Prior to the development of sprinklers, furrow irrigation was the most popular method on the Great Plains. Farmers frequently used siphon tubes to supply each furrow from the head ditch. The tubes enabled better control than when the ditch was cut open, and it reduced bank erosion. This farmer irrigated his land near Riverton, Wyoming, in July 1941. (Courtesy of the Nebraska State Historical Society)

The flooding technique simply required a worker to open the bank of a head ditch. The water then irrigated the relatively level field. A ridge or border along the edge confined the water to the field. (Courtesy of the Kansas State Historical Society)

In 1926, this farmer in Scottsbluff County, Nebraska, used the furrow method to irrigate his potato field. He drew his water from the Farmer's or Tri-State Canal. (Courtesy of the Nebraska State Historical Society)

Even on the relatively level High Plains, good irrigation often depended upon additional leveling of the land. Some areas, however, were sufficiently level to enable ditch irrigation without special preparation. This farmer irrigated his sugar beets with the furrow method in eastern Colorado. (Courtesy of the Colorado Historical Society)

During the 1940s, sprinkler irrigation enabled farmers to forego the expense of digging ditches and leveling land. Pipe carried the water from the pump to the field. This sprinkler system irrigated a newly planted apple orchard near East Wenatches, Washington, in June 1947. (Courtesy of the Shields Library, University of California-Davis)

began in 1880 with the construction of 12 irrigation canals along the Arkansas River in the southwestern portion of the state. Farmers also used shallow wells to ensure a water supply when the river ran low. As a whole, though, Kansas farmers were slow to develop the state's irrigation resources. By 1929, only 71,290 acres of a potential 1.3 million acres were irrigated. Although farmers were generally interested in irrigation, the agricultural depression of the 1920s discouraged the required investment for such endeavors. Small-scale irrigation cost as much as $25 per acre — a prohibitive expense at that time. As a result, irrigation was available at low cost only to those farmers who lived along streams or in the flood plains of the larger rivers.[14]

The drought of the 1930s, however, convinced Kansas farmers that irrigation would stabilize, if not increase, crop production. Farmers in southwestern Kansas were the first to invest heavily in irrigation technology for crop insurance because the water table was close to the surface, therefore drilling and pumping costs were manageable. During the 1930s, farmers with pumping plants produced near normal harvests while dryland crops approached a complete failure. Moreover, irrigation increased land values. One farmer in western Kansas claimed the $100 to $200 per acre cost of irrigation was more than offset by the increase in land values — often as much as $250 per acre.[15]

After 1936, extension of the natural gas fields to provide energy for the pumps enabled irrigation to expand farther into the Kansas high plains and away from the alluvial river valleys and shallow water basins. Where irrigation stabilized agricultural production, crops such as hay increased in value, while new crops of alfalfa and sugar beets boosted farm income. By the end of the decade some farmers believed irrigation meant the difference between crop failure and a profitable year. Near Scott City, for

example, 85 pumping plants enabled farmers to irrigate approximately 15,000 acres with production diversified among truck, feed, and alfalfa crops. Irrigation became a stabilizing factor for these farmers and the general economy of southwestern Kansas.[16]

By the late 1930s, farmers all across the Kansas plains became interested in irrigation, and they gradually extended pumping plants from west to east much in contrast to the directional flow of other agricultural technology, such as the steel plow, reaper, and binder. Still, in 1939, most of the state's irrigation was centered in southwestern Kansas, where the sandy loam soil proved ideal for irrigation. The number of wells in that region had increased from 614 to 1,351 during the decade; nearly half of them had been sunk after 1933.[17]

The farmers in southwestern Kansas found irrigation with ground water more reliable than surface water because it was less subject to drought. When streams dried up, the wells usually had water for irrigation. As a result, the irrigation farmer who depended upon well water became independent of the weather, and drought no longer posed a hazard — at least while pumping rates did not greatly exceed annual recharge. At first, however, few farmers worried about the depletion of the ground water supply. Although the Kansas State Geological Survey investigated the ground water reserves in western Kansas during 1933, it could not determine the rate of recharge nor ascertain the total amount of water at depths ranging from 20 to 70 feet. Although the agency urged caution in developing ground water resources for irrigation, it contended the water supply was sufficient to warrant additional expansion. With that report, most concerns about the water supply temporarily vanished.[18]

In the Kansas plains farmers learned that by irrigating traditional dryland crops, such as wheat and sorghum, they could expand production. Irrigation did not mandate

Sprinklers enabled farmers to irrigate moderately rolling land without causing soil erosion. The aluminum pipe could be coupled and uncoupled relatively easily. The nearly constant winds of the Great Plains often caused greater losses to evaporation than by ditch irrigation. (Courtesy of the Kansas State Historical Society)

Single nozzle sprinklers can be adjusted to permit the appropriate amount of water to be spread across a field. Low application rates keep evaporation to a minimum where wind velocities are high. (Courtesy of the University of Missouri Agricultural Extension, photo by Duane Dailey)

High-pressure nozzles enable farmers to irrigate a wide area at each "set." This water-powered, gear-driven sprinkler can be moved easily. (Courtesy of the University of Missouri Agricultural Extension, photo by Duane Dailey)

new cropping practices, such as sugar beets or potatoes, which required a considerable investment for labor. Still, by 1949, only 2.8 percent of the total crop acres in southwestern Kansas were under irrigation, and those acres constituted nearly 93 percent of the irrigated acreage in the state. Only 12 percent of the irrigated lands in southwestern Kansas had been leveled primarily because costs remained high — $30 to $50 per acre. As a result, farmers frequently wasted water, particularly where it could be withdrawn cheaply from streams, and less than 10 percent of these lands were properly irrigated.[19]

During the 1950s, irrigation expanded rapidly in Kansas for several reasons. First, the drought returned with severity across the Great Plains for most of the decade, and farmers and scientists alike feared the return of another Dust Bowl. Farmers again turned to irrigation to ensure a profitable harvest during the drought years. Second, irrigation systems became more convenient with the introduction of aluminum and gated pipe and easily movable sprinkler systems. Third, Kansas farmers increasingly used commercial fertilizer. Drought tended to burn crops after high application rates of nitrogen fertilizer, and irrigation alleviated that problem. Fourth, many farmers could afford the average cost of $7,000 for the installation of a well, pump, motor, pipe, and sprinklers. Put differently, costs averaged $15 per acre, but irrigation increased productivity and profits. In 1954, for example, irrigation increased the per acre yields of alfalfa 2.4 tons, forage sorghums 9.5 tons, grain sorghum 22 bushels, and wheat 11 bushels. Compared to total costs that easily reached as high as $50 per acre for leveling land for ditch irrigation, sprinklers were a bargain.[20]

Problems

The return of drought during the 1950s and 1970s fostered the increase in irrigation across the Kansas plains. During the 1980s, however, farmers and scientists gave greater consideration to the depletion of the underground water supply. Farmers not only dug deeper wells, with depths averaging more than 300 feet in southwestern Kansas, but they also pumped more water than ever before. In northwestern Kansas farmers used 100 wells to

High-pressure nozzles particularly are useful in areas where wind velocities are low. Here, a Missouri farmer irrigates a soybean field with his sprinkler system. (Courtesy of the University of Missouri Agricultural Extension, photo by Duane Dailey)

pump 15,000 acre-feet in 1950; by the mid-1970s they used 2,250 wells to pump 500,000 acre-feet annually. Consequently, the water table dropped 36 feet in some parts of that area and several wells reached 800 feet by 1958. Since that time, the water table has continued to drop, sometimes more than a foot each year.[21]

In western Kansas the Ogallala formation provides most of the ground water for irrigation, but recharge is slow because the water is restored from precipitation, seepage from streams, and inflow from surrounding areas. The recharge rate is hampered by high summer temperatures, low humidities, and strong winds. Recharge of the aquifer also depends on vegetative cover, land slope, and soil permeability. The amount of recharge varies from one-quarter inch annually in southwestern Kansas to six inches annually in east-central Kansas. Because irrigation is heaviest in the area of Kansas that receives only 16 to 18 inches of precipitation annually, water mining remains a serious problem.[22]

Even though ground water reserves continue to decline in the Kansas plains, irrigation has changed traditional agricultural practices. Prior to the mid-1950s, for example, few farmers risked planting corn west of the Flint Hills in eastern Kansas. By the early 1970s, however, irrigated corn had replaced dryland feed crops in many western Kansas fields, and yields reached more than 200 bushels per acre. Irrigation also has changed the livestock industry, because it enabled cattlemen to feed more livestock during drought. In Kansas, for example, irrigation farmers produced nearly half of the corn in the state and one-third of the grain sorghum by 1967. Because irrigation assures a stable harvest of these crops, cattlemen in irrigated areas increasingly expanded their livestock feeding operations. Dryland farmers, who fed 30 to 40 head of livestock during the mid-1950s, could feed 150 to 250 head per year with the aid of irrigation a decade later. Moreover, irrigation supported the development of large-scale commercial feedlots in western Kansas. In 1968, 100 feedlots with a

capacity of 1,000 head operated in the state, and 26 of those feedlots were located in southwestern Kansas. Without irrigation these feedlots would have incurred additional, if not prohibitive, expenses from supplying feed grains trucked from outside the area. By the late 1960s, the use of irrigation, hybrid feeds, and fertilizer helped rank Kansas eighth in the livestock-feeding industry.[23]

Irrigation agriculture required considerable hand labor to move the first sprinkler systems. During the 1960s, labor shortages on the Great Plains made the expensive, center-pivot sprinklers attractive. Electric motors or water turbines power these sprinklers as the system pivots around the well in the center of the field. (Courtesy of the Lindsay Manufacturing Company)

Irrigation in Kansas also boosted sorghum seed, sugar beet, and fertilizer sales. Prior to irrigation, farmers restricted the application of fertilizer to wheat acreage; however, high yields from various irrigated crops quickly depletes the soil and necessitates the application of additional fertilizer. Consequently, the numbers of fertilizer distributors, irrigation equipment manufacturers, and sales representatives have increased in irrigated areas. Because irrigation boosts income, it also has increased the tax revenue of the state. In 1966, for example, irrigation farmers in Kansas raised their income about $33 for each acre-foot of water applied to their fields. Two years later, economists estimated the state received at least $10 for every acre-foot of water used and that farm income increased about $26 million because of irrigation. Moreover, a 1968 survey of four counties in southwestern Kansas indicated the price paid for irrigated land averaged $121 compared to $80 per acre for dryland. In 1976, the price of irrigated land averaged $740 compared to $476 for nonirrigated farm land and $264 per acre for ranch land. Still, operating costs remained high. By the late 1970s, a Kansas farmer could expect to invest between $30,000 and $50,000 for well and pumping plant. Yet, many farmers made that investment. By 1987, irrigated farm land in Kansas, like other agricultural acreage, had declined in value. But, it still averaged $549 per acre

The center-pivot sprinkler system has nozzles located along the length of pipe that carries the water to the field. The system rotates and irrigates the crop according to a predetermined rate. Evaporation losses can be high, but the water is essential for corn, sugar beet, and alfalfa crops west of the 100th meridian. (Courtesy of the Lindsay Manufacturing Company)

Valmont Industries of Valley, Nebraska, manufactured one of the earliest center-pivot systems. Here, Valley sprinklers irrigate moderately rolling land. Center-pivot sprinklers enabled farmers to irrigate land too rough for the furrow method and to turn submarginal acreage into highly paying crop land. (Courtesy Valmont Industries, Inc.)

Center-pivot sprinklers have changed the look and the use of the land in the High Plains. West of the 100th meridian the circles of these systems are readily apparent from the air. (Courtesy of Valmont Industries, Inc.)

compared to $404 per acre for dryland.[24]

Conclusion

Irrigation technology, like the cotton picker, spread from the West Coast to the Great Plains. Certainly, irrigation has reduced the drought hazard for those farmers who have access to an adequate supply of ground and surface water. Irrigation enables farmers in humid and semiarid regions to provide supplemental or "insurance" water to their crops during critical periods of growth or when precipitation drops below normal, thereby stabilizing or increasing production. Moreover, without irrigation commercial agriculture in the arid West would be impossible. Cheaper methods for drilling wells, technological developments that permit irrigators to pump water from increasingly greater depths, and center-pivot sprinklers are responsible for the expansion of irrigation in the West.[25]

Sprinkler irrigation, however, causes some problems. It requires more labor once the system is set up than ditch irrigation, because the pipes must be skidded or wheeled to change locations at the proper time, unless it is an automated system such as center-pivot. Workers are required to couple and uncouple pipe and move it during the course of a day to new locations or "sets." On the Great Plains high winds and temperatures and low humidities cause water loss to evaporation and uneven water applica-

tion by the sprinkler method. In addition, sprinklers can become awkward in tall growing crops, such as corn and forage sorghum. In the West, however, sprinkler irrigation has been advantageous where the land is too rough or shallow to permit leveling for flooding or gravity methods. Sprinkler irrigation also has become the most effective technique on porous soils that lose water during gravity irrigation or where the water supply was insufficient or too slow for surface irrigation methods.[26]

By the mid-1970s, center-pivot systems became the most common sprinkler method for the irrigation of field crops. Center-pivot systems could travel on 30 percent grades, although this sprinkler performed best when the grade did not exceed 10 percent. The height of the center-pivot system did not interfere with the growing crops, and farmers could adjust the application rate of the water as well as precisely apply fertilizer and pesticides while irrigating. All of these advantages made the center-pivot system attractive to irrigation farmers and to those agriculturists who wanted to develop unimproved or marginal lands. On the Great Plains center-pivot systems provide the most efficient irrigation method, and it has changed the use of the land in many areas from wheat and sorghum to corn, alfalfa, and livestock production.[27]

Consistently high yields, however, are necessary to offset irrigation expenses, and the cost of failure is high.

Moreover, planning is required to prepare the land for gravity irrigation, for choosing the best sprinkler system, and for selecting the proper seed varieties and fertilizer amounts as well as for claiming one's legal right to limited water supplies in the West. Historically, irrigation has not been a cure-all for agriculture in the West. And, where farmers have relied on irrigation for more than crop insurance, the depletion of ground water has encouraged some of them to return to dryland agriculture.[28]

Certainly, irrigation improves crop conditions, helps stabilize agricultural productivity and boosts income. But, irrigation also lowers the protein content of wheat. To overcome this problem farmers must apply great quantities of nitrogen per acre. Heavy irrigation and the application of fertilizer and water, however, causes other problems. The concentration of salt or alkali in the soil results from insufficient leaching of these minerals while the chemicals that filter through the soil damage drinking water supplies. Often the results are sterile lands or farms with decreasing productivity as well as a public health hazard. Farmers also pay higher taxes on irrigated than nonirrigated farm and ranch land. In some areas of the West, they also must pay for the water that they use. Even so, counties with extensive irrigation on the Texas high plains have stabilized or increased in population.[29]

By 1990, some irrigation farmers in California and Arizona had reduced their water use by half while doubling their yields. They did so by delivering water, pesticides, and fertilizer to their orchards drip by drip via underground plastic pipe. Although few farmers were interested in this subsurface technology, it offered substantial savings from the loss of water to evaporation by ditch or sprinkler methods or from runoff. Subsurface irrigation also retards weed growth between the rows. Experiments indicate that productivity increases with subsurface drip irrigation compared to other irrigation methods. Tomatoes, for example, increased from 26 to 100 tons per acre while cotton jumped from 930 to 1,600 pounds per acre. Cost, however, remains prohibitive. A farmer spends about $275 per acre annually for subsurface irrigation compared to $55 per acre for furrow irrigation. Whether increased yields together with reduced water use and tillage will save farmers enough money to merit the additional $220 investment remains to be proven.[30]

As the twenty-first century nears, irrigation will continue to play an important role in the agricultural history of that region, but that is rather obvious. More to the point, irrigation has affected the social, legal, political, and economic systems of the West. In the future, the technical and economic problems of irrigation farmers may become less significant while the social and environmental concerns of urbanites, expressed by law and politics, may dictate the use of water in the West. During the 1970s and 1980s, for example, some ditch irrigation companies in southeastern Colorado sold their water rights to cities, such as Colorado Springs and Denver, because farming was too uncertain and unprofitable and because these cities needed the water. The rapid growth of the urban West may cause problems for irrigation farmers that technology cannot solve.[31]

NOTES

1. D. W. Thorne and H. B. Peterson, *Irrigated Soils* (Philadelphia: The Blakistan Co., 1949), 2: Andrew B. Erhart, "How Far for Irrigation in Kansas?" *Thirty-Eighth Biennial Report of the Kansas State Board of Agriculture* (1951-1952): 25; Willard D. Johnson, "The High Plains and Their Utilization," U.S. Geological Survey, Twenty-First Annual Report, 1899-1900, pt.4, *Hydrology*, 611; R. Douglas Hurt, *Indian Agriculture in America: Prehistory to the Present* (Lawrence: University Press of Kansas, 1987), 21-22.

2. L. H. Bailey, *Cyclopedia of American Agriculture*, vol. 1 (New York: Macmillan Co., 1907), 428.

3. Donald E. Green, *Land of the Underground Rain: Irrigation on the Texas High Plains, 1910-1970* (Austin: University of Texas Press, 1973), 40-46, 61, 118.

4. *Ibid.*, 125-131, 143-144, 163-164, 233.

5. Leslie Bowen, "Irrigation of Field Crops on the Great Plains," *Agricultural Engineering*, 19 (Jan. 1938): 13-14; Bailey, *Cyclopedia of American Agriculture*, 433; John C. Steele, "Water Application Methods," *Nebraska Irrigation Statistics, 1945-1948* (Lincoln: State-Federal Division of Agricultural Statistics, n.d.), 65-66.

6. Andrew B. Erhart, Walter R. Meyer, and Ben L. Glover, "Irrigation in Western Kansas," Kansas Agricultural Experiment Station, *Circular 324* (1955), 9-10; Steele, "Water Application Methods," 66; Bowen, "Irrigation of Field Crops," 14.

7. Steele, "Water Application Methods," 66; Erhart, Meyer and Glover, "Irrigation in Western Kansas," 10-11; George D. Clyde, "Irrigation in the West," *Yearbook of Agriculture, 1943-1947*, 605.

8. Allan W. McCulloch and John F. Schrunk, *Sprinkler Irrigation* (Washington, D.C.: Sheiry Press, 1955), 170.

9. *Ibid.*, 118, 185.

10. Clyde, "Irrigation in the West," 606; Steele, "Water Application Methods," 66; Guy O. Woodward, *Sprinkler Irrigation* (Washington, D.C.: Darby Printing Co., 1959), 12, 14-15.

11. Bert S. Gittins, *Land of Plenty* (Chicago: Farm Implement Institute, 1959), 45; McCulloch and Schrunk, *Sprinkler Irrigation*, 1, 14.

12. William E. Splinter, "Center-Pivot Irrigation," *Scientific American* 234 (June 1976): 90, 93; Rollie E. Deering, "Understanding Pivot Sprinklers," *Farm Quarterly*, 24 (Spring 1969): 94.

13. Russell Herpich, "Sprinkler Developments in Kansas," *Irrigation Age*, 5 (Jan. 1971): 18; "1973 Irrigation Survey," *Irrigation Journal*, 8 (Nov.-Dec. 1973): 14.

14. Erhart, "How Far for Irrigation in Kansas," 26; M. H. Davison, "Irrigation and Stabilized Agriculture," *Thirty-First Biennial Report of the Kansas State Board of Agriculture* (1937-1938): 80-81; "Land Available for Agriculture Through Reclamation," *Supplementary Report of the Land Planning Committee to the Natural Resources Board*, part 4 (Washington, D.C.: Government Printing Office, 1936), 12; "Report of the Division of Water Resources," *Twenty-Seventh Biennial Report of the Kansas State Board of Agriculture* (1929-1930): 280; R. V. Smrha, "Irrigation for Crop Insurance," *Twenty-Eighty Biennial Report of the Kansas State Board of Agriculture* (1931-1932): 139.

15. Davison, "Irrigation and Stabilized Agriculture," 89; G. W. Pepoon, "Irrigation Success in Kansas," *Twenty-Ninth Biennial Report of the Kansas State Board of Agriculture* (1933-1934): 105; J. W. Lough, Scott City, KS, to the Farm Credit Administration, 3 June 1933, National Archives, Record Group 103.

16. "Deep Well Pumping Plants," *Report of the Kansas State Board of Agriculture 57* (Sept. 1938): 5; *Garden City Daily Telegram*, 8 June 1937; Harry R. O'Brian, "Water for the Earth," *Country Gentleman*, 111 (Jan. 1941): 16, 42.

17. George S. Knapp, "Report of the Division of Water Resources," *Thirty-First Biennial Report of the Kansas State Board of Agriculture* (1937-1938), 148; L. Carl Brandhorst, "The North Platte Oasis: Notes on the Geography and History of an Irrigated District," *Agricultural History*, 51 (Jan. 1977): 166; Richard Pfister, *Water Resources and Irrigation*, Economic Development of Southwestern Kansas, pt. 4 (Lawrence: University of Kansas School of Business, Bureau of Business Research, Mar. 1955), 65, 69; Hal F. Eier, "Irrigation in Kansas," *Kansas State Engineer*, 22 (Feb. 1940): 4; "Irrigation in Kansas," *Progress in Kansas*, 6 (Sept. 1940): 258.

18. "Irrigation Pumping Plants: Construction and Cost," *Report of the Kansas State Board of Agriculture*, 61 (Oct. 1942): 6; Rycroft G. Moss, "Preliminary Report on Ground Water Resources of the Shallow Water Basin in Scott and Finney Counties, Kansas," 1 Oct. 1933, *Circular 5* (Lawrence: State Geological Survey of Kansas), 1, 6, 7, mimeographed, National Archives, Record Group 103.

19. "Growth of Irrigation in Scott County, Kansas," *Report of the Kansas State Board of Agriculture*, 63 (Aug. 1944): 18, 22, 24; Pfister, *Water Resources and Irrigation*, 79, 81, 84-85; Russell L. Herpich, "Kansas Irrigation Potential," *Forty-Second Annual Report of the Kansas State Board of Agriculture* (July 1958-June 1959): 51; Richard E. Hanson, "Irrigation Requirements: Estimates for Kansas," Kansas State College, Engineering Experiment Station, *Bulletin 69* (15 June 1953): 3.

20. *The Topeka Capital*, 14 June 1953, 29 June 1958; John J. Penney, John A. Anderson, and Donald F. Kostechi, *Little Arkansas River Basin*, Kansas Water Resources Board, State Water Plan Studies, part C (1975), 30-31; Merton L. Otto and Wilfred H. Pine, "Sprinkler Irrigation Costs and Returns: South-Central Kansas," Kansas Agricultural Experiment Station, *Bulletin 381* (1956), 3, 4, 13.

21. Andrew B. Erhart, "Irrigation Activity Looks Up Throughout Southwestern Kansas," *Kansas Business Magazine*, 21 (July 1953): 46; Marilyn E. Pabst and Edward D. Jenkins, *Water-Level Changes in Northwestern Kansas, 1950-1973* (Lawrence: Kansas Geological Survey and U.S. Geological Survey, 1973), 1-2; Danny D. Trayer, "An Economic Analysis of Irrigation with a Limited Supply of Water in Southwest Kansas," (Master's thesis, Kansas State University, 1967), *Kansas Farmer*, 115 (16 Apr. 1977): A.

22. Pabst and Jenkins, Water-Level Changes in Northwestern Kansas, 2; R. H. Griffin, II, B. J. Ott, and J. F. Stone, "Effects of Water Management and Surface Applied Barriers on Yields and Moisture Utilization of Grain Sorghum in the Southern Great Plains," *Agronomy Journal*, 58 (July 1966): 449; Pfister, *Water Resources and Irrigation*, 16; Eier, "Irrigation in Kansas," 14; *Kansas State Water Plan Studies: Long Range Water Supply Problems Phase I*, Bureau of Reclamation in cooperation with the Kansas State Water Resources Board (Oct. 1974), 28; *The Wichita Eagle-Beacon*, 22 Oct. 1972.

23. Jerry Fetterolf, "Blue Water and Green Fields," *Kansas!* (1973), 10; Personal observation of the Author; Interview with Orval Harold, Area Conservationist, Soil Conservation Service, Manhattan, KS, Spring 1976; "Irrigating Agricultural Land," *Monthly Review*, Federal Reserve Bank of Kansas City (Apr. 1945), 9; Harold

24. Shankland and Russell L. Herpich, "Kansas Turns to the Second Century," *Reclamation Era*, 47 (Aug. 1961): 76; *1964 U.S. Census of Agriculture, Kansas*, 58, 90, 140; "Kansas Water News," *Irrigation Age* 2 (Sept. 1967): 50; Huber Self, "Irrigation Farming in Kansas," *Transactions of the Kansas Academy of Science*, 74 (Fall/Winter 1971):314-315; *Topeka Journal*, 16 Aug. 1967; *Topeka Journal, Midway Magazine*, 18 Feb. 1968.

24. *Kansas Farmer*, 15 Mar. 1976, 5 Feb. 1977; Shankland and Herpich, "Kansas Turns to the Second Century," 76-77; Nelda C. Thomas, "Management Emphasized on Tour in Kansas," *Irrigation Age*, 4 (Oct. 1970): 20-21; Erhart, "How Far for Irrigation in Kansas," 32; David D. Darling, *Economic Implications of Irrigation: A Pilot Study*, Bulletin no. 9 (Kansas Water Resources Board, 1968): 3-4; Samuel H. Lee, "The Effects of Underground Water Supply on Land Values in Southwestern Kansas (Master's thesis, Kansas State University, 1968), 54; *1987 Census of Agriculture: Kansas*, 16-17.

25. Brandhorst, "The North Platte Oasis," 166; Pfister, *Water Resources and Irrigation*, 3.

26. Green, *Land of the Underground Rain*, 194; Pfister, *Water Resources and Irrigation*, 86; Ivan D. Wood, "Irrigation in the Middle West," *Agricultural Engineering*, 38 (June 1957): 419; Woodward, *Sprinkler Irrigation*, 3.

27. Splinter, "Center-Pivot Irrigation," 94, 96.

28. Erhart, "Irrigation in Western Kansas," 5; Lee, "The Effects of Underground Water Supply on Land Values in Southwestern Kansas," 2; "1973 Irrigation Statistics," 14; Otto, "Sprinkler Irrigation Returns," 8; Vance Ermke, "Pre-Irrigated Milo Can Top Corn," *Successful Farming*, 75 (Feb. 1977): F21; Bill Gergen, "New Efforts to Conserve Irrigation Water," *Successful Farming*, 75 (Mar. 1977): L16-17.

29. Donald Grimes, George M. Herron, and Jack T. Musick, "Irrigation and Fertilizing Winter Wheat in Southwestern Kansas," Kansas Agricultural Experiment Station, *Bulletin 442* (1962), 8-9; Green, *Land of the Underground Rain*, 163; O'Brian, "Water for the Earth," 42; L. Carl Brandhorst, "The Panacea of Irrigation: Fact or Fancy," *Journal of the West*, 7 (Oct. 1968): 507; Erhart, "Irrigation in Western Kansas," 5.

30. *Des Moines Register*, 14 Jan. 1990.

31. James E. Sherow, "Utopia, Reality, and Irrigation: The Plight of the Fort Lyon Canal Company in the Arkansas River Valley," *Western Historical Quarterly*, 20 (May 1989): 180.

Chapter 5

Mechanizing the Sugar Beet Harvest

THE sugar beet crop, like cotton, remained one of the last field crops to be completely mechanized in the twentieth century. Unlike cotton, however, the mechanization of the sugar beet harvest occurred relatively quickly. Indeed, a mechanical harvester became practical within a decade of the first extensive experimental work which began in the mid-1930s. By the early 1950s, the sugar beet harvest had been completely mechanized. Yet, like the cotton crop, the complete mechanization of the sugar beet harvest required more than just the invention of a machine. It required the improvement of planters and cultivators and the development of a new seed.[1]

Although the Great Western Sugar Company in Denver offered a large cash prize in 1913 to the first person who developed a successful sugar beet harvester, no one met that challenge. More than 50 inventors entered their machines in the competition, but only 15 proved meritorious for field testing, and a viable mechanical sugar beet harvester was not among them. Further innovation lagged until the early 1920s when sugar beet farmers began using horse-drawn seed drills, cultivators, and lifters (diggers) to speed and ease the labor of these tasks. Farmers also adopted mechanical loaders to lift and elevate the beets from a pile or windrow, via an endless belt, into a truck or wagon. "Stoop" labor still was required to lift, windrow, and top the beets before the crop could be hauled to the sugar factory. Even with these modest improvements, about 85 man-hours were required to produce an acre of sugar beets as late as 1922.[2]

Sugar beet farmers sought to mechanize their production for the same reasons that cotton and wheat farmers hoped for the development of mechanical pickers and harvesters. They wanted to ease their labor, reduce the time needed to harvest their crops, and to decrease or eliminate labor costs, particularly after the United States Department of Agriculture (USDA) required a minimum wage for sugar beet workers in 1937. At that time, approximately 78 man-hours per acre still were required for preparing the land, planting the crops, thinning the seedlings, hoeing the weeds, digging and topping the crops, and loading the beets for the factory at harvest time. In California, the harvest crews averaged 8 to 15 workers. Large crews, however, were sometimes difficult to find. In sugar beet areas that experienced cold weather by harvest time, such as Michigan, Montana, and Minnesota, migrant laborers frequently moved South to work in warmer weather before the beets were ready to harvest. Consequently, harvest labor often was expensive, inadequate, or in short supply, and sugar beet farmers looked forward to the development of a mechanical harvester to end this annual logistical problem.[3]

Early Developments

In 1931 the California Agricultural Experiment Station

Sugar beet production required considerable hard work prior to mechanization of the crop. Labor peaked twice each year — once in the spring during the blocking, thinning, and weeding season and again during the harvest season in the autumn. These men, women, and children hoed sugar beets in Colorado near the turn of the twentieth century. (Courtesy of the Colorado Historical Society)

(CAES) together with the USDA began work to mechanize sugar beet production. The major sugar beet processors, such as Utah-Idaho Sugar Company, also gave advisory and financial support. After 1938 the U.S. Sugar Beet Association aided this effort by providing $114,000 for research, and it gave additional support for similar work at Colorado State University. This research led to the mechanical blocking, thinning, and harvesting of the crop.[4]

During the 1930s, agricultural engineers experimented with harvesters that would lift, top, and load the beets in one operation. The two most difficult problems involved topping the beets and removing the clods and trash from the beets. One sugar beet harvester, tested in 1938, saved a Mexican topping crew about one-third of their time by lifting the beets from the soil and piling them for topping. A year later, several experimental topping machines scalped the leaves and left only two or three inches of stem which enabled the field workers to build larger piles of sugar beets. This improvement enabled easier topping by hand for a similar labor savings of one-third. These machines, however, usually topped large beets too high and small beets too low.[5]

Workers used a knife with a long blade to top sugar beets. The hook at the end enabled the harvester to pick up the beets without bending all the way over. This woman worked in a beet field near Fisher, Minnesota, in October 1937. At that time, about 30 hours of labor were needed to pull, top, and load an acre of sugar beets. (Courtesy of the Farm Security Administration, photo by Russell Lee)

Sugar beets have heavy foliage and deep roots. A lush crop, such as this near Billings, Montana, *ca.* 1911, was harvested by hand. The development of a successful mechanical harvester required the joint efforts of plant breeders and agricultural engineers. (Courtesy of the Minnesota Historical Society)

New innovations, however, did not eliminate the need for "stoop" labor by the late 1930s. By 1938 agricultural engineers focused their attention on the perfection of two types of sugar beet harvesters that would help eliminate more hand labor. One machine topped the beets in the ground then lifted the roots and separated the clods, leaves, and other trash from the beets on a cleaning device. The second type of experimental harvester lifted the beets and passed the roots to a gauge and knife combination that removed the tops. The gauge on the first harvester consisted either of a wheel, endless track, sliding finger, or shoe that traveled down the beet row. As the gauge moved up or down a knife behind it topped the beets. This technique did not work efficiently, and it made agricultural engineers devote their attention to passing the beets through a gauging device and power knives after the harvester had lifted the roots from the ground. Topping within the harvester also damaged the leaves less and helped retain their value as cattle feed. Despite these imperfections, field tests in California and Colorado during the 1935 season proved that mechanical harvesters performed as well as and sometimes better than migrant workers.[6]

Between 1938 and 1943, J. B. Powers, an agricultural engineer at the CAES, solved the topping problem after he discovered a relationship between beet diameter and crown thickness. He then developed a topping mechanism that automatically adjusted to the size of each beet.

Despite these modest but encouraging results, it was the labor shortage during World War II which ultimately stimulated the mechanization of the sugar beet harvest. During World War II, many agricultural engineers at the implement manufacturers, the agricultural experiment stations, and the USDA attempted to build a mechanical harvester. The result was the development of several sugar beet harvesters that proved satisfactory by the end of the war.[7]

Breakthrough

The sugar beet harvesters that underwent testing in California and the Midwest during the 1940s were of four types: Each was a "once-over" machine that topped, lifted, and windrowed or loaded the beets in a single operation. The first harvester offered for commercial sale was a single-row machine. It topped the beets in the ground and windrowed the leaves and beets. Then, a separate loader lifted the beets onto a truck. The second type of harvester had a large spike wheel which lifted the beets while topping chisels and sickles severed the leaves. A roller-screen removed the dirt and elevated the leaves to a truck. The third type of harvester utilized hand labor to sort the clods and leaves from the beets. This machine topped the beets in the ground, lifted, cleaned, and elevated the roots to a sorting table, then into a truck. The fourth type of sugar beet harvester was a single-row unit that plowed the beets and lifted them by the tops. Then, the harvester elevated the beets into the machine for topping and delivery to a truck. The tops fell to the ground in a row. This machine was most popular in Michigan and Ohio where it harvested approximately 7 percent of the crop in 1946.[8]

In California the two most popular machines were the two-row, spike-wheel harvester and the one-row, hand-sorting harvester. The two-row, spike-wheel harvester had a pair of wheels, six feet in diameter, with closely spaced spikes around the rim. As the harvester moved down a plant row behind a tractor, a blade undercut the beets and loosened them sufficiently for the spikes to spear and lift them from the ground. Then, the beets passed across a cutting disk or chisel that removed the tops and dropped the beets onto cleaning rollers and a conveyor belt that carried them to a truck that moved alongside the harvester. The tops fell onto another conveyor which deposited them in a windrow. The machine required a 50- to 60-horse-power track-type tractor for draft power for most field conditions. A 60- to 80-horsepower track-type tractor,

Prior to World War I, approximately 128 man-hours were needed to produce an acre of sugar beets. When this photograph was taken about 1940 in the Red River Valley of the North, the labor required had been reduced to about 97 hours, because of mechanical planting and lifting implements. (Courtesy of the Minnesota Historical Society)

Prior to mechanization, harvesting consisted of digging, topping, and loading the beets into trucks for hauling to the sugar refinery. First, the farmer used a plow to cut under the roots and lift them to the surface. Then, crews of 8 to 15 workers pulled the beets and cut off the tops. In 1922, these children helped their parents top beets and place them in a pile for pickup. At that time, 116 man-hours were required to produce an acre of sugar beets. (Courtesy of the Kansas State Historical Society)

however, proved more satisfactory if the ground was hard, or if the crop was particularly heavy. An auxiliary gasoline engine powered the working parts of the harvester, such as the topping disks, sickles, cleaning rollers, and conveyors. Harvesting with the two-row, spike harvester required one man to operate the tractor and another to operate the machine. This implement could harvest 6 acres with a 17-ton yield in a 9-hour day. With harvest time beginning in early September and ending in mid-November in California, these sugar beet machines could be employed about 50 days or on about 250 acres during the season. Muddy fields, however, usually brought this harvester to a halt because of its weight.[9]

Most California growers, however, who did not raise 50 acres of sugar beets annually could not meet the initial investment of approximately $5,500 for a two-row, double-spike harvester. Harvesting costs per acre increased rapidly when the beet production fell below 250 acres. With 50 acres in production, mechanical harvesting costs averaged $25.04 per acre compared to $39.67 per acre by hand. Growers who raised fewer than 50 acres of sugar beets were better off hiring a custom harvester, thereby avoiding the investment and repair costs of an expensive technology. Moreover, some growers resisted mechanical harvesting because the two-row machine damaged the tops of the sugar beets. Many growers sold their beet tops to cattle feeders in the form of pasture rights, and they did not want to lose any supplementary income. Generally, losses due to crushed or dirty leaves averaged $3.40 per acre. Still, this loss only increased harvesting costs to $17.13 per acre for a 250-acre crop. The total savings of mechanical harvesting over hand harvesting averaged approximately $23 per acre. Most growers were happy with this savings if their economy of scale permitted investment in a mechanical harvester or the hiring of a custom crew.[10]

In 1948 California growers also tested the one-row, hand-sorting harvester. Engineers mounted this harvester on a general-purpose tractor. This design reduced costs, because the tractor could be used for other work throughout the year. The one-row, hand-sorting harvester topped the beets with a rotating scalloped disk. Then, rotating steel fingers removed the foliage from the disk and dropped the leaves in a windrow beneath the tractor's wheels. A lifter with two blades raised the beets and guided them to a cleaning roller where the dirt vibrated off. Then, the beets rose to a sorting belt above the bin where one or two workers, standing on a platform, removed the last of the clods, leaves, and weeds that had passed over the cleaning rollers. Next, the beets dropped into a bin. The one-row, hand-sorting harvester so efficiently collected beets that hand harvesters and gleaners were not needed to follow the machine over the field. Because the beet tops dropped between the tires of the tractor and cart, they were not severely damaged for grazing purposes.[11]

The one-row, hand-sorting harvester required a 25-horsepower tractor for greatest efficiency and an investment of $2,274. A farmer could harvest 125 acres during a 55-day harvest season, or 2.5 acres in a 10-hour day based on a yield of 17 tons per acre. At these rates the machine could harvest at a cost of $18.19 per acre for a savings of $21.48 over the hand-harvesting cost of $39.67 per acre. With a savings such as this, a grower could afford to mechanize the harvest when he raised 25 acres of sugar beets. At that point, harvest costs averaged $29.93 per acre. These monetary savings enabled California growers to reap greater profits, particularly when the beet yield and the sugar content of the roots remained low. Increased profitability from mechanization, however, did not cause great expansion of sugar beet production in California, because most growers did not have the extra acreage.

Moreover, they believed that they could not raise sugar beets on the same land more frequently than every three or four years.[12]

The Midwest

The efforts to mechanize the sugar beet harvest, however, were not limited to California. East of the Rocky Mountains, as early as 1936, mechanical engineers also experimented with sugar beet harvesters. By 1943 Deere & Company had 32 machines in operation. These harvesters lifted, topped, and piled beets in windrows for pick up by another machine. In 1948 Deere had 2,600 machines available for the harvest. At this same time, International Harvester Company (IHC) also experimented with several machines, the most successful of which also involved a two-step process. This machine lifted and topped the beets, and a loader channeled the roots onto a conveyor where workers removed the clods and trash by hand. The beets were then elevated and dropped into a truck pulled alongside. By 1949 IHC had 2,700 hand-sorting machines in operation. This limited success encouraged mechanical engineers to consolidate these two operations and thereby eliminate pick-up and hand-sorting tasks.[13]

In Michigan, agricultural engineers were most successful with a machine tested in 1945. This harvester cut under the beets with a blade and lifted the roots between two rotating disks which removed the leaves. The tops then fell behind the harvester while a conveyor elevated the beets to

In October 1942, agricultural engineers at the University of California at Davis demonstrated the first successful sugar beet harvester. This harvester topped the beets at ground level with a knife and lifted the roots on a spiked wheel which deposited them on a conveyor for delivery into a truck. A powerful, track-type tractor with at least 50 to 60 horsepower was required to pull these harvesters. (Courtesy of the Shields Library, University of California-Davis)

Some growers used mechanical loaders to pick up the sugar beets after the crop had been lifted, topped, and deposited in windrows by hand labor. This machine deposited the beets into a truck for delivery to the refinery. (Courtesy of the Colorado Historical Society)

John Deere & Company began building a one-row sugar beet harvester in 1943. Those machines delivered six or eight rows of beets and three or four rows of tops into a windrow. A field loader elevated the crop into a truck. In 1951, this John Deere harvester lifted, topped, and loaded the beets in one operation. One man rode the harvester to separate the clods that passed through the cleaning device. (Courtesy of the Colorado Historical Society)

an accompanying truck. This machine did not harvest the entire crop, and gleaners had to follow the harvester. Similarly, sugar beet harvesting had gone somewhat beyond the experimental stage in Nebraska by 1947. At that time, farmers used 30 "topper-pullers," but this machine severely damaged the tops and reduced the value of the leaves for cattle feed.[14]

By the early 1950s, demand for sugar beet harvesters exceeded supply. Sugar beet harvesters became particularly popular among farmers who contracted with the Utah-Idaho Sugar Company's Columbia Basin plant. In fact, growers used so many harvesters that the company proclaimed its beets were "untouched by human hands." Improvements on the machines enabled additional labor

reductions for sugar beet production. By the mid-1960s, only 2.7 man-hours were required to produce a ton of beets in contrast to 11.2 man-hours during World War I — a time savings of more than 75 percent. By the early 1970s, sugar beet farmers could purchase harvesters which ranged in size from one to six rows. The largest machines could harvest 24 acres per day or 500 tons in a ten-hour day. With hydraulic power from large tractors, sugar beet harvesters could operate in all but the muddiest fields. They now were "all weather" machines.[15]

Custom Harvesting

Not every sugar beet farmer could afford a mechanical harvester. When machine harvesting became widespread

By 1959, growers commonly used sugar beet harvesters in the Red River Valley of Minnesota. Nationwide, 20,000 mechanical harvesters gathered the entire crop. Labor shortages after World War II provided the stimulus for sugar beet growers to mechanize. (Courtesy of the Minnesota Historical Society)

This John Deere harvester uses two rotating and converging wheels to loosen each row of beets and lift them from the ground and into a topping and cleaning mechanism. A rod-type elevator carries the beets from the bin to a truck. (Courtesy of the U.S. Sugar Beet Association)

in the Southern San Joaquin and Imperial Valleys and along the California coast in 1945, the sugar companies owned most of the harvesters in operation. The farmers were reluctant to make the large capital investment in an unproven technology. The sugar companies, however, rented harvesters to the growers in an attempt to encourage them to mechanize. Improper operation and poor maintenance proved unsolvable problems. Mechanization also lagged because the farmers often planted double rows of beets, but they did not own tractors powerful enough to pull double-row harvesters. Custom harvesters, however, soon alleviated these problems.[16]

Custom harvesting enabled the small-scale grower, who could not afford his own machine, to complete his harvest quicker and cheaper than with hand labor. Based on a yield of 17 tons per acre, hand-harvesting costs averaged $2.33 per ton in California during the 1940s, while custom-harvesting rates averaged only $1.65 per ton. Custom harvesters preferred the two-row machines because this equipment was durable and well-suited for large-scale operations. Some custom-harvester operators got maximum use from their machines by beginning the sugar beet harvest in the Imperial Valley during the spring. Then, they moved to the coastal areas and to the interior valleys by the autumn.[17]

Related Improvements

Although complete mechanization of the sugar beet crop became possible by 1950, many other aspects of sugar beet production remained unmechanized. By the late 1940s, workers still used a hoe to thin and block the crop. Although growers had used a beet-seed drill as early as 1923 to improve planting uniformity at a consistent depth, hand labor was required for all other tasks of sugar beet production. After the seeds sprouted, for example, workers used a hoe to "block" the beets, that is, chop out all of the beets in a row except for groupings spaced about a foot apart. Then, another worker pulled the remaining seedlings except one. Although a horse-drawn cultivator could clear the weeds between the rows, workers with long-handled hoes weeded between the sugar beet plants. When the leaves of the beets shaded the ground sufficiently to prevent weed growth, the hand labor ceased.[18]

By 1941, engineers at the CAES had developed a mechanical cross-blocker. It had a series of knives that rotated at right angles to the row. As the cross-blocker moved down the row, the fingers rotated and removed the beets except for predetermined blocks that were gauged

The complete mechanization of the sugar beet crop involved cultivation as well as harvesting. Although farmers used horse-drawn cultivators by the 1920s, tractors provided the necessary power for 12-row rigs by 1950. (Courtesy of the United States Department of Agriculture)

mechanically. Farmers quickly adopted the mechanical cross-blockers, because they could use their cultivators for this purpose with only a few minor and inexpensive adjustments. Mechanical cross-blockers enabled one man to block seven acres per day instead of one-half acre by hand. This labor savings particularly was significant to sugar beet growers when labor remained scarce or when the weather delayed hand blocking. Still, mechanical cross-blocking required uniform rows of beets. And, if germination was low, mechanical cross-blockers left many sections in a row without beets.[19]

The delay in the mechanization of blocking, thinning, and harvesting is attributable to the nature of the beet seed. The sugar beet seed was a multigerm ball, varying in size from 1/8 to 1/4 inch in diameter. Each ball contained many seeds or germs, and it produced dense clumps of seedlings. Because sugar beet seeds were not uniform in size, seed drills often did not plant uniformly and gaps in the rows resulted. Low rates of germination also prevented the most efficient mechanical blocking and thinning. To solve these problems which limited mechanical development, growers needed a monogerm seed. As in the case of cotton and tomatoes, complete mechanization only became possible when scientists changed the seed.[20]

In 1941 Roy Bainer, an engineer at the CAES, discovered that sugar beet seed balls had specific cleavage or shear lines. He believed these cleavage points would enable the seed ball to be split into single-germ segments, and he began experimenting with a machine that cut the seed ball into parts. Bainer's success with segmenting sugar beet seeds proved an important achievement. His machine used a rotating silicon-carbide stone or emery wheel that carried the seed past a sheer bar. This shearing process broke the seed into small parts or "segments." Bainer's technique, however, damaged the seed and further experiments led to the "decorticating" process which involved rubbing off the corky material around the seed germ. The resulting product was called "processed" seed. By the early 1950s, 90 percent of the sugar beet acreage had been planted with processed seed that either had been segmented or decorticated. Farmers preferred processed seed because it produced a uniform crop that was well suited for mechanical blocking, thinning, and cultivating. They also wasted less seed at planting time. Before processed seed, for example, farmers planted 18 to 20 pounds of seed per acre. With segmented or decorticated seed, however, they only needed six to eight pounds per acre.[21]

In addition, processed seed eliminated at least 10 hours per acre for hand thinning for an estimated saving of 5 million man-hours, during a peak labor period. Hand thinning, however, had not been eliminated entirely, because farmers overseeded to ensure against losses due to poor germination. Nevertheless, with segmented seed achieving 60 to 90 percent germination by 1944, mechanical thinning became practical.[22]

In 1956 V. F. Savitsky, a scientist with the Sugar Beet Development Foundation in association with the USDA, succeeded in developing a monogerm seed. First planted commercially in 1957 for nearly 4 percent of the crop, nearly 100 percent of the sugar beet crop grew from monogerm seeds a decade later. The development of monogerm seed enabled farmers to depend on precision planting and germination rates as high as 90 percent compared to 60 percent germination rates for multigerm seeds. With this achievement, together with the development of a reliable harvester, the man-hours required to produce a ton of sugar beets dropped from 40.8 in 1948 to 2.7 by 1964.[23]

Conclusion

Not all sugar beet growers favored mechanization during the 1940s. In areas where farmers raised potatoes, beans, and other truck crops in addition to sugar beets, a mechanical harvester threatened to eliminate a labor supply that farmers needed for their other crops. Moreover, growers who relied on beet tops to generate income as livestock feed also resisted mechanization, because forage losses sometimes reached 75 percent of the leaf value for a monetary loss of more than $40 per acre. Labor shortages during and following World War II, however, quickly changed their minds, particularly among Montana growers where adequate harvest labor always had been difficult to obtain. At this same time, growers became increasingly dissatisfied with the migrant labor programs of the federal government. Indeed, this technology freed them from the bother of securing migrant labor crews and providing them with rudimentary shelter and care. With the mechanical harvester, the growers could complete the harvest with family labor, with a custom-harvesting crew or local, nonmigrant labor which, in the parlance of the day, they termed "regular" labor. With the perfection of the mechanical harvester and other technological improvements by the early 1950s, no sugar beet grower advocated a return to the past when hand labor prevailed. The harvester did not threaten the social order in the manner of the cotton picker, and no opposition contested this technological improvement. Economics and the development of a reliable harvester relegated hand labor to the past and changed sugar beet farming for all time.[24]

NOTES

1. S. W. McBirney, "New Sugar Beet Machinery," *Yearbook of Agriculture, 1943-1947*, 851; Russell T. Johnson, ed., *Advances in Sugar Beet Production: Principles and Practices* (Ames: Iowa State University Press, 1971), 386; *The Sugar Beet Story* (Washington, D.C.: U. S. Beet Sugar Association, 1959), 232; O. A. Holtervig, "Experiments With Non-Thinning of Sugar Beets," *Proceedings of the American Society of Sugar Beet Technologists, 1940*, pt. 1, 262; Roy Bainer, "Sugar Beet Harvester Tests 1938-1939," *Ibid.*, 274-282.

2. Austin A. Armer, "Historical Highlights in Sugar Beet Harvest Mechanization," *Journal of the American Society of Sugar Beet Technologists*, 13 (Jan. 1965): 318-319, 325; Wayne D. Rasmussen, "Technological Change in Western Sugar Beet Production, *Agricultural History*, 41 (Jan. 1967): 32; Warren R. Bailey, "Economics of Sugar-Beet Mechanization in California," United States Department of Agriculture, *Circular 907* (1952), 2; H. L. Stewart, "Some of the Farm Economic Aspects of Sugar Beet Mechanization," *Proceedings of the American Society of Sugar Beet Technologists, 1950*, 688.

3. R. H. Cottrell, ed., *Beet Sugar Economics* (Caldwell, ID: Caxton Printers, 1952), 183, 192; Bailey, "Economics of Sugar-Beet Mechanization in California," 1-2.

4. Rasmussen, "Technological Change in Western Sugar Beet Production," 32.

5. S. W. McBirney, "Development and Performance of Single Seed Sugar Beet Planters," *Proceedings of the American Society of Sugar Beet Technologists, 1940*, pt. 1, 252-253.

The combination of improved seed and better planters helped produce a uniform crop well suited for mechanical blocking, thinning, cultivating, and harvesting. (Courtesy of the U.S. Sugar Beet Association)

6. E. M. Mervine, "Developments in Mechanical Equipment and Methods in Sugar-Beet Production," United States Department of Agriculture, *Circular 488* (1938), 2-35.

7. Leonard J. Arrington, *Beet Sugar in the West: A History of the Utah-Idaho Sugar Company, 1891-1966* (Seattle: University of Washington Press, 1966), 152; Bailey, "Economics of Sugar-Beet Mechanization in California," 2.

8. G. W. Howard, "Results of Survey of Sugar Beet Harvester Performance," *Proceedings of the American Society of Sugar Beet Technologists, 1946*, 509-513; Stewart, "Some of the Farm Economic Aspects of Sugar Beet Mechanization," 688; McBirney, "New Sugar-Beet Machinery," 853-854.

9. Bailey, "Economics of Sugar-Beet Mechanization in California," 16-22.

10. *Ibid.*, 6-9, 27-29.

11. *Ibid.*, 31-33.

12. *Ibid.*, 9-11, 34, 36, 48.

13. Howard, "Results of Survey of Sugar Beet Harvester Performance," 509-510; Johnson, *Advances in Sugar Beet Production*, 387-388.

14. C. M. Hansen, L. E. Smith, and R. W. Bell, "Sugar-Beet Harvester Trails in Michigan in 1945," *Quarterly Bulletin of the Michigan State Agricultural Experiment Station*, 28 (May 1946): 340; James E. Rowan, "Mechanization of the Sugar Beet Industry of Scottsbluff County, Nebraska," *Economic Geography*, 24 (July 1948): 175.

15. Arrington, *Beet Sugar in the West*, 153; Johnson, *Advances in Sugar Beet Production*, 38.

16. C. C. O'Hara, "Custom Harvesting in California," *Proceedings of the American Society of Sugar Beet Technologists, 1952*, 620.

17. *Ibid.*, 620-621; Bailey, "Economics of Sugar-Beet Mechanization in California," 39.

18. Cottrell, *Sugar-Beet Economics*, 126; Rasmussen, "Technological Change in Western Sugar Beet Production," 31-32.

19. Arrington, *Beet Sugar in the West*, 114, 144.

20. McBirney, "New Sugar-Beet Machinery," 851; Rasmussen, "Technological Change in Western Sugar Beet Production," 33.

21. Arrington, *Beet Sugar in the West*, 145-146; Cottrell, *Sugar-Beet Economics*, 183-184; McBirney," New Sugar-Beet Technology," 852.

22. Arrington, *Beet Sugar in the West*, 146-147.

23. Rasmussen, "Technological Change in Western Sugar Beet Production," 35.

24. *Ibid.*, 33; James R. Mason, "The Mechanical Harvesting of Beets and Tops in the Great Western Territories," *Proceedings of the American Society of Sugar Beet Technologists, 1952*, 625-626, 629; Bailey, "Economics of Sugar-Beet Mechanization in California," 9.

Chapter 6

Tomato Harvesters: From West to East

WORLD War II created the demand among growers and processors for a mechanical tomato harvester. High wartime prices and an inadequate labor supply encouraged agricultural engineers to develop a machine that could harvest the crop quickly and eliminate the grower's dependence on migrant workers, who picked the fields three or four times at intervals of one or two weeks. Tomatoes, however, posed greater problems for the development of a mechanical harvester than most crops. The vines, for example, easily jammed moving parts, and the fruit did not reach maturity uniformly. Moreover, thin-skinned tomatoes bruised and cracked easily, which meant economic loss because the processors paid lower prices for damaged fruit.[1]

Although the crop for processing tomatoes is centered in California while Florida provides most of the market-fresh crop, other states are important producers. In fact, the first mechanical efforts to speed the tomato harvest came in Pennsylvania where a farmer by the name of

Garber used a hammock contraption that extended from the sides of a truck. Each hammock held a picker who reached over the plants and plucked the fruit as the truck traveled down the rows. A conveyor belt carried the tomatoes to the truck. Some growers used this winged device during the harvest seasons of 1941 and 1942. Other efforts were just as cumbersome and unsuccessful, because mechanical tomato harvesters of every design ruined the plants. Indeed, tomato harvesters have been once-over machines from the beginning, that is, these harvesters destroy the plants while removing the fruit. Growers did not have a second, third, or fourth opportunity to harvest all of the tomatoes in the field. Consequently, losses were high because processors could not use green fruit.[2]

The complicated nature of tomato production led to a "systems approach" in which agricultural engineers, horticulturists, and agronomists pooled their collective talents to build a mechanical harvester as well as breed a tomato that could withstand machine harvesting. As a result, they

Tomato growers in California relied on cheap, migrant labor at harvest time before termination of the bracero program in 1964. Because the tomato plants did not set or ripen fruit uniformly, workers had to pick the field several times. By the early 1960s, growers looked forward to a mechanical harvester that would eliminate most of their labor-supply problems. (Courtesy of the Smithsonian Institution)

Tomatoes destined for the family table require considerable care during harvest and transport to market. The successful development of a mechanical harvester for market-fresh tomatoes required the breeding of new varieties that could withstand mechanical picking without greater damage than by hand picking. These biological and technological problems were not resolved until the late 1970s. (Courtesy of the Smithsonian Institution)

developed new tomato varieties that set and ripened uniformly and that resisted bruising and cracking during rough, mechanical handling. They also changed planting, cultivating, and irrigating practices — all of which made mechanical harvesting possible.[3]

Upon the development of the mechanical harvester, tomato processors gave their support by adjusting production schedules to meet the large quantity of fruit delivered at one time. The processors also lowered their purchasing standards to accommodate the growers who used the new varieties and technology. This subsidization by the processors encouraged growers to adopt or expand their planting of the new tomato varieties and to use mechanical harvesters. As a result, between 1961, when growers first used the mechanical harvester commercially, and 1967, when they picked virtually the entire crop mechanically, the machine-harvested acreage increased more than 90 percent while the number of implements increased 80 percent. Indeed, the systems approach enabled the scientific and technological problems of the tomato harvest to be solved relatively quickly compared to other crops such as cotton. In California, for example, 30 years passed from the introduction of the cotton picker until growers mechanically harvested the entire crop, while only six years were required to achieve the same success in the tomato fields.[4]

Early Experiments

California led the nation in the systems approach that resulted in the development of a commercially successful tomato harvester. The University of California at Davis pioneered this work in 1943 when G. C. Hanna began plant breeding experiments designed to produce a tomato that would survive mechanical picking. In 1959, after more than a decade of work, Hanna produced a tough-skinned, pear-shaped tomato. This variety "set" most of its fruit at the same time and held it for about 30 days without deterioration. These advantages enabled the tomatoes to

In 1959, scientists and agricultural engineers at the University of California at Davis and the Blackwelder Manufacturing Company of Rio Vista, California, built the first successful tomato harvester. This machine destroyed the vines in a "once-over" harvesting process. Consequently, growers had to use new tomato varieties that set and ripened uniformly to ensure maximum profits and yields. (Courtesy of the Shields Library, University of California at Davis)

ripen before harvesting. Consumers, however, rejected pear-shaped tomatoes for the table. Consequently, this fruit was suitable only for processing into catsup, juice, or paste, because food manufacturers could tolerate some bruising and cracking, if they processed the fruit quickly. Cultural and aesthetic preferences, then, relegated the pear-shaped tomato, which was the only fruit that could withstand mechanical harvesting, to the processing industry.[5]

The tomato plant breeding experiments, however, enabled agricultural engineers to proceed with their efforts to develop a mechanical harvester. In 1949 this work began in earnest, when Colby Lorenzen, an agricultural engineer at the University of California at Davis, joined Hanna to solve the technological problems involved with mechanical harvesting. Lorenzen accepted the limiting principal that a mechanical harvester of any type would destroy the plants, and he worked to produce a once-over machine. Lorenzen experimented with a number of lifting and cutting devices that removed the tomatoes from the vines, sorted the ripe and near-ripe fruit from the green tomatoes, clods, and trash that entered the machine and conveyed the fruit to a bin or truck drawn alongside. Lorenzen labored on this project for a decade before his harvester was ready for testing on Hanna's tomatoes in 1959.[6]

Once the tomato harvester had been successfully tested,

the University licensed it to the Blackwelder Manufacturing Company for commercial production. At the same time, other inventors experimented with tomato harvesters. The Davis machine, however, received the most publicity, in part because it worked better than the other models and because the University had a professional public relations office to publicize its success. Although only 1,200 tons of tomatoes were harvested mechanically under experimental conditions in 1959, the Blackwelder Manufacturing Company had 25 machines in the fields for the harvest in 1961. Even so, these machines, together with a few others, harvested less than 1 percent of California's tomato crop that year.[7]

Nationwide Developments

While the experiments continued in California, agricultural engineers at other state universities engaged in tomato harvester work. In 1958, for example, engineers at Michigan State University built a mechanical harvester, which they improved during the next three years. By 1961, private inventors and implement companies had also joined the various university efforts to build a mechanical harvester. The H. D. Hume Company, the FMC (Food Machinery Corporation), and the Ziegenmeyer Company developed harvesters, while a grower, Robert L. Button, Jr., built a machine and licensed it to the Benner Nawman

Company in California. A year later, the Massey-Ferguson Company entered the field with a mechanical harvester.[8]

All of the mechanical tomato harvesters developed during the early 1960s worked on the same basic principles. When most of the tomatoes had ripened, the harvesters traveled down the rows, severed the plants about or slightly below ground level with a sickle, V-shaped blade, or rotating disk, and lifted the vines and fruit to an elevator which carried them to a shaking device where the tomatoes dropped from the vines. Agricultural engineers at Michigan State University developed the shaking mechanism incorporated in most harvesters to remove the fruit from the vines. This device consisted of a bed that reciprocated with a four-inch stroke at the rate of 175 to 200 cycles per minute. The vines fell to the ground, and the tomatoes dropped onto a conveyor which carried the fruit to a sorting area where workers, walking along, removed the green tomatoes, clods, trash, and severely damaged fruit before the ripe tomatoes dropped into a bin drawn alongside for transport to the processing plants.[9]

Practicality, however, did not mean perfection or commercial viability. These early harvesters frequently damaged even the tough, pear-shaped tomato, collected dirt,

knocked the fruit to the ground, lacked sufficient capacity, or needed frequent repairs. By 1966, however, most of these problems had been solved, and growers mechanically harvested approximately 70 percent of the California crop, thereby eliminating an estimated 3.5 million man-hours of labor annually. Losses averaged 15 to 20 percent, or about that encountered when hand labor harvested the crop. By 1970, however, machines had not completely mechanized the harvest because hand sorters were required to remove the green fruit and trash from the ripe tomatoes. Moreover, market-fresh or table tomatoes remained a crop that required hand labor.[10]

Complete mechanization also lagged because of economic as well as technological problems. By 1965, for example, mechanical harvesting became economically feasible only when a grower reaped at least 30 tons per acre. In addition, almost all of the tomatoes had to be uniformly ripe and undamaged upon arrival at the processors. Most growers could not meet these requirements, except in California. As a result in 1966, California growers used 760 of the 771 tomato harvesters in operation nationwide. This concentration and rapid adoption of the mechanical harvester indicates that growers in California found these implements advantageous and profitable.[11]

Growers used the Blackwelder mechanical harvester, based on the University of California's design, to pick pear-shaped tomatoes. This machine harvested at the rate of 10 tons per hour on a 30-ton per acre crop. (Courtesy of the Shields Library, University of California at Davis)

The Blackwelder tomato harvester severed the vine near ground level with a cutter bar. An elevator consisting of belts and metal fingers lifted the plant onto a shaking mechanism similar to the straw walkers in combines. The fruit fell onto another conveyor that delivered it to inspectors. A third conveyor carried the fruit to a truck or bin drawn alongside. (Courtesy of the Shields Library, University of California at Davis)

Indeed, the mechanical harvester picked more tomatoes at less cost than hand labor. By 1965, harvest crews in California picked an average of .35 tons of tomatoes per hour while a good, individual worker could only pick .19 tons per hour. These rates meant that 113 man-hours were required to harvest an acre of tomatoes that yielded 21.5 tons. In contrast, the mechanical harvester could perform that work in 61 man-hours for a savings of 52 man-hours per acre. Machine harvesting costs averaged $9.84 per acre compared to hand labor that cost as much as $17.19 per acre for a savings of $7.35 per acre. At this same time, growers worried about the unionization of migrant workers and periodic shortages of hand labor. Confronted with these savings and problems, the growers readily converted to mechanical harvesters.[12]

The mechanization of the tomato harvest continued to lag in the Midwest and East during the 1970s. By 1973 growers had mechanized only 30 percent of the harvest in these areas. Here, precipitation during the harvest season often kept the heavy harvesters from the fields, because these implements easily mired in the clay, silt, and sandy loam soils. With a 45-day harvest season in Indiana, for

example, a mechanical picker could be used for only about 30 days, because of wet weather. Decreased efficiency because of soil type and precipitation raised the break-even point and decreased net profits. Simply put, soil and climate posed problems that technology could not overcome.[13]

Market-fresh Tomatoes

The mechanization of the tomato crop destined for the table proved more difficult. Indeed, by the late 1980s, the problems of mechanization associated with the fresh-market crop had not been completely solved. Because consumers continued to demand a round, tender, juicy tomato, plant breeders had difficulty developing a tough-skinned variety with these characteristics that could endure rough, machine harvesting. During the mid-1960s, when the problems of mechanical harvesting for processing tomatoes essentially had been solved, research teams applied the systems approach to the mechanization problems of fresh-market tomatoes in Florida.[14]

The growers in Florida envied the tomato producers in California who had decreased their harvesting costs from

$18 to $6 per ton by 1970. The Florida growers wanted similar savings at harvest time and freedom from the annual uncertainties about the labor supply and the threat of cheap foreign competition. At the University of Florida, specialists formed a state-wide research team to develop new varieties and cultural practices as well as a mechanical harvester. In 1969, Norman Hayslip, at the University of Florida's Indian River Field Laboratory at Ft. Pierce, and William Deen, at the Everglades Experiment Station at Belle Glade, tested their "once-over" harvester. This harvester severed the plants below the ground with a diagonal blade, lifted the vines with rubber-

In 1980, this mechanical harvester deposited tomatoes into a tractor-drawn trailer for delivery to a processor that would convert the crop into catsup, juice, and paste. (Courtesy of the United States Department of Agriculture)

In California, growers primarily raise processing rather than market-fresh tomatoes. These sorters ride the mechanical harvester and remove the vines, rocks, clods, and green tomatoes before the conveyor lifts the crop onto a truck driven alongside. (Courtesy of the United States Department of Agriculture)

covered fingers, and shook the tomatoes from the plant. A conveyor located beneath the shaker carried the leaves, vines, and soil out of the machine. The tomatoes rolled down another conveyor into a 100-gallon water tank for cleaning. Although this machine worked fairly well, it still handled the fruit too roughly and with more damage than hand harvesters. It also failed to separate adequately the fruit from the collected vines, clods, and rocks. Several harvester tests by other agricultural engineers met with similar limited results.[15]

In 1970 the Food Technology Corporation of Reston, Virginia, helped develop a mechanical harvester at Clemson University. This tractor-mounted harvester cut and elevated the plants and separated the tomatoes from the vines on an oscillating conveyor. The fruit collected in bins. Field tests on tomatoes that had not been planted for mechanical harvesting proved difficult, because many of the vines were too widely spaced, the rows were too dense, or the plant beds or ridges were too high. Further tests of the Clemson harvester indicated that additional work was required to perfect the implement, because this machine reduced the harvest as well as the price paid for the tomatoes. In fact, the harvester damaged the crop so much that a grower could expect a net loss of nearly $136 per acre compared to a net gain of $1,000 per acre by hand harvesting. Confronted with these gloomy results, the Clemson scientists began work to develop a tomato variety that would increase yields sufficiently to offset the economic loss from mechanical harvesting.[16]

With the failure of the Florida and Clemson harvesters, agricultural engineers gave increased attention to modifying the tomato harvesters designed for the processing crop. And, by 1972, researchers at the University of Florida had developed a "semi-harvester" which they hoped would help growers meet foreign competition and encourage them to adopt mechanization. This machine, when used in conjunction with the university's new MH-1 tomato (MH-1 meant machine harvesting), reduced harvest labor costs between 50 and 75 percent under field tests. This new Florida machine enabled a dozen workers to harvest 30 tons of tomatoes each day — a job that usually required between 30 and 40 laborers. With a selling price of $10,000, this machine seemed cheap compared to $150,000 implements used in California. Two other machines developed at this time, however, cost as much as $30,000.[17]

The Florida machine and the MH-1 tomato variety were important components of the systems approach to the development of a mechanical harvester that could pick, sort, and wash market-fresh tomatoes without bruising or cracking the fruit. With the Florida tomato crop valued at $100 million annually, the growers anxiously awaited a mechanical harvester that would enable them to "neutralize" cheap Mexican tomatoes. Indeed, by 1970, Mexican imports had increased more than 220 percent over the previous decade. With workers in Mexico paid about $2.10 for a ten-hour day in the tomato fields, Florida growers

The tomato harvester eliminated four of the five workers needed to harvest a crop by hand. These pear-shaped tomatoes were especially bred to withstand the relatively rough handling of the mechanical harvester. (Courtesy of the United States Department of Agriculture)

could not compete with those substantially lower production costs, because hourly labor rates in Florida exceeded the daily wages in Mexico. The Florida growers hoped that a mechanical harvester would be developed soon to handle their market-fresh crops. Like the harvesters built for processing tomatoes, however, success depended on the joint efforts of plant breeders and agricultural engineers.[18]

This systems approach took time. By 1970 plant breeders had worked to develop a "jointless" tomato that would separate easily from the stem. The jointless varieties eliminated the problem of the stems puncturing the fruit during mechanical handling. The plant breeders also made hundreds of genetic experiments to ensure the maintenance of tastiness, redness, disease resistance, maturity, and skin thickness for tomatoes destined for machine harvesting. Moreover, some scientists experimented with various chemical sprays to retard plant growth and, thereby, improve separation of the fruit from the vine and to speed the maturation and a uniform set of the tomatoes.[19]

Mechanical harvesting became even more important for the growers in Florida during the mid-1970s, because their production increased rapidly to 33,000 acres for a gross return of $141 million by the 1976-1977 growing season. High labor costs and a shortage of workers caused the growers to fear lost profits from crops that potentially might be left in the field. Still, a viable mechanical harvester for market tomatoes had not yet been perfected. The major problem remaining involved cultural practice. About 75 percent of the Florida growers used plastic to cover their tomato beds or rows, and the plastic invariably became tangled in the mechanical harvesters. Although one of the more successful machines, a Button-Johnson harvester, had been fitted with a special cutter that severed the tomato plant above the plastic sheet mulch, this implement remained an experimental device at mid-decade.[20]

In June 1974 scientists at the University of Florida tested an improved model of the Clemson tomato harvester. It collected the fruit on a conveyor after the vines had been cut and allowed to wilt for as much as eight hours. This machine utilized a vertical and horizontal shaker and a chlorinated water spray to wash the fruit and help prevent decay. The harvester picked the fruit with about the same degree of injury as hand harvesters. By pre-cutting the vines, the growers reduced the soil intake and decreased the damage to the fruit while they increased the life of their machinery. Wilting also enabled better separation and removal of the fruit. These features, when combined with the proper variety, bed preparation, and plant density, eliminated the most serious problems for mechanically harvesting market-fresh tomatoes. Technological and scientific development, together with changed cultural practices, made mechanical harvesting of market-fresh tomatoes possible by the late 1970s. During the 1978-1979 harvest season, five machines harvested a portion of the crop in Florida.[21]

By the early 1980s, tomato growers, however, still preferred to use hand labor for the first and second pickings, when prices were high. Then, they used the tomato harvester for the third and final picking. They preferred this management technique, if hand labor was adequate and affordable, because buyers reduced the price for bruised, scratched, or cracked tomatoes. Although scientists and agricultural engineers worked to improve both the mechanical harvester and the tomato, hand harvesting still produced better results. Hand harvesting also was faster than the mechanical harvester. Moreover, mechanical harvesting required carefully calculated planting schedules and selection of the best varieties to permit the fruit to reach the mature green stage at once. In addition, this process required the grower to make smaller and more frequent plantings in order to control the harvest and shipment to market.[22]

Labor Displacement

The mechanical tomato harvester like the mechanical cotton picker contributed to large-scale technological displacement. Indeed, thousands of workers lost their jobs. By the mid-1960s, mechanical harvesters could harvest the tomato crop in California for $5.41 per ton, while

"stoop" labor cost $7.47 per ton. With the savings of $2.06 per ton, growers had the economic incentive to mechanize. By 1970, growers mechanically harvested 95 percent of the California crop.[23]

The rapid mechanization of the tomato harvest in California was largely stimulated, however, not by per acre or tonnage cost savings, although that was an important consideration, but rather as a means to resolve a perceived labor shortage problem after the termination of the bracero program in 1964. In the Midwest, however, mechanization resulted from the efforts of the growers and processors to defeat unionization by migrant workers. Although the unionization of agricultural workers in California began decades before the 1960s, not until 1968, with the creation of the Farm Labor Organizing Committee (FLOC), did the growers and processors in the Midwest take a serious interest in mechanical tomato harvesters.[24]

Indeed, mechanization appealed to Midwestern growers and processors alike because it offered the potential to eliminate strikes and boycotts by migrant workers. The cost savings at harvest time were merely an added benefit. In 1969 FLOC, led by Baldemar Velasquez and patterned after the United Farm Workers union in California, targeted the large-scale growers and used the strike to gain improved contracts. By 1974, FLOC had won more than 30 contracts among the growers in Ohio, which guaranteed minimum wages and improved living and working conditions. All of the tomato growers in Ohio, however, were contract farmers and therefore tied inextricably to the processors. The growers had little financial flexibility to meet the increased salary and benefit demands of the workers, because their earnings had been determined long before harvest time by the price that the processor contracted to pay. As a result, FLOC often made economic demands that growers believed they could not meet. Consequently, many of the growers ended their tomato production.[25]

After failing to win union recognition from the growers, FLOC targeted the processors. In 1978 FLOC struck the fields that had been contracted by Campbell's Soup Company and Libby's, then went on strike again in 1979 and 1980. These processors reacted by forcing their contract growers to adopt mechanical pickers to ensure adequate and timely delivery of the crop at harvest time. The processors not only required machine harvesting but they also gave contracts for larger acreages to those growers who adopted the mechanical harvester. More acreage meant greater production and greater profits. The growers did not have any choice in Ohio. If they wanted to raise tomatoes, they needed a market, and to gain a market they needed a contract. In order to get a contract, the grower had to promise to mechanize his harvest. The processors, then, not the growers, broke the organizational back of FLOC in the Midwest, and they used the mechanical harvester to do so.[26]

Certainly, the mechanical harvester displaced many workers, who had to look elsewhere for seasonal employ-

These tomatoes are bound for a processor in California. Because consumers insisted on round tomatoes for the table, plant breeders had to develop such a tomato that could withstand machine harvesting. By the late 1970s, they had solved this problem for Florida growers, who produced a market-fresh crop. (Courtesy of the United States Department of Agriculture)

ment, and it forced some farmers to adopt other crops. In 1977, for example, 4,500 migrant workers harvested the tomato crop for 88 growers in Putnam County, Ohio. By 1980 only 44 growers remained who hired 1,000 workers. Whether their lives improved because of this forced dislocation and readjustment remains unknown. The immediate effects, however, were family uncertainty, economic hardship, and changed patterns in the movement of migratory labor. In this respect, the mechanical harvester clearly proved to be in the best interests of the food manufacturers, but not of the growers, because hand labor remained cheaper. During the early 1970s, for example, Ohio growers earned a net return of $107 per ton by mechanical harvesting compared to nearly $113 per ton by hand harvesting. This increased profit from hand harvesting resulted because workers could pick the fields several times to collect the late ripening fruit.[27]

For the Midwestern growers, who remained in business, the mechanical harvester produced lower yields than that garnered from hand harvesting. In the mid-1970s, hand harvesting yielded 27 tons per acre in Ohio while machines harvested only 24.6 tons per acre. Based on these results, researchers at Ohio State University concluded that the investment in a mechanical harvester was unwarranted if hand harvesting produced two or more tons per acre above machine picking. Still, mechanization im-

proved the economy of scale for the large-scale producers. They recovered their losses due to price reductions for mechanical harvesting by expanding their acreage beyond the 50 acres needed to merit mechanical harvesting.[28]

Although mechanization based on calculation replaced migrant workers in the Ohio tomato fields, the University of California rather than the processors has been viewed as the villain regarding technological displacement on the West Coast. Largely due to the cooperative efforts of the scientists and agricultural engineers at the University of California at Davis, the tomato harvester reduced the number of hand pickers nationwide from 50,000 in 1963 to 18,000 by 1970. In California, the number of hand harvesters decreased over that same period from 38,000 to fewer than 8,000 workers. By the early 1990s, most of the remaining field workers were women, who rode the mechanical harvesters and sorted the trash and unripened fruit from the tomatoes destined for the processors.[29]

Although the mechanical harvester clearly reduced the number of workers needed at harvest time, no one can be certain whether the tomato harvester eliminated jobs in California. Prior to 1964, the bracero program brought large numbers of Mexican workers into the United States and the tomato fields at harvest time. This program began in 1942 for the purpose of bringing temporary Mexican workers into the United States under federal or private contract. The federal government intended the bracero program to alleviate emergency labor shortages. The growers, however, used these migrant workers to keep wages low and the labor supply plentiful. When Congress ended this degrading and inhumane program in 1964, the mechanical harvester was ready for adoption to replace that foreign labor supply. Moreover, mechanization encouraged large-scale production which created work for additional irrigators, implement operators, and cannery workers. At the same time, population growth, affluence, and health concerns have stimulated the labor-intensive production of fruits and vegetables. As a result, 192,000 farm workers were employed in California in 1960 and 224,000 in 1980. Moreover, the workers who remain in the tomato fields at harvest time have easier work because of the mechanical harvester. Certainly, the mechanical tomato harvester eliminated much of the stooping and lifting in the tomato fields and, thereby, lengthened the working lives of those who remained. Moreover, the development of new plant varieties along with the mechanical pickers have lengthened the harvest season, because it can be calculated with greater accuracy.[30]

The tomato harvester has not decreased the need for workers in the California fields. Hand harvesting still is required for grapes, citrus and deciduous fruits, fresh tomatoes, lettuce, and other vegetables. In California alone manual labor accounted for 56.6 percent of the 189 million man-hours needed to harvest the $7.1 billion truck crops in 1976. By the mid-1980s, hand labor remained essential to agriculture in California, and to help meet their needs growers hired between 200,000 and 300,000 illegal aliens annually.[31]

Conclusion

Although agricultural engineers experimented with the tomato harvester as early as 1959, hand labor essentially picked the entire processing crop before 1964. When the bracero labor program terminated, the growers sought mechanization to replace this cheap source of harvest labor. Growers were so concerned about the loss of their labor supply that many feared the tomato industry would shift to Mexico. By the end of the decade, however, machines harvested virtually all of the processing tomatoes in California. In the Midwest, the processors used the mechanical harvester to prevent the growth of a strong union among migrant workers.[32]

In California, the mechanical harvester also encouraged growers to expand production. Between 1964 and 1974, for example, the tomato acreage increased from 159,183 to 259,308 acres. Tomato harvesters, of course, did not increase yields per acre but these implements reduced harvesting costs by substituting capital for labor. Only the large-scale growers, however, could afford the $150,000 tomato harvesters, and small-scale growers could not compete with those who purchased these machines. As a result, the tomato harvester helped decrease the number of growers nationwide while it helped increase the acreage

planted. In 1982, for example, 17,290 growers produced tomatoes, but five years later, only 14,290 growers remained. And, in 1987, growers harvested 375,470 acres, more than double the 1964 figure. Mechanization helped make expansion possible, but history seldom is influenced by a single cause. In the case of tomato production, the completion of the irrigation system in the San Joaquin Valley encouraged growers to specialize in tomato production and to convert other agricultural lands to this farming endeavor.[33]

The development of a satisfactory harvester for other regions took more time than in California, where mild climatic conditions prevailed. In Pennsylvania, for example, the relatively short, wet growing season and small-scale farms presented problems. In contrast, the dry climate of California as well as large-scale farms made mechanization convenient and economical. In California growers could plant several varieties to stretch the harvest season over six or eight weeks and, thereby, increase tonnage and profits while reducing unit costs. Not until the mid-1970s did growers east of the Mississippi River have varieties that enabled them to extend the season and withstand rough machine harvesting. Similarly, the development of a mechanical harvester for market-fresh tomatoes took more than a decade beyond the perfection of a machine for harvesting tomatoes designed for processing.[34]

The systems approach to the mechanization of the tomato harvest combined basic and applied scientific research. The results of that research have aided the large-scale growers and the processors while eliminating most small-scale farmers and migrant workers from tomato production. Certainly, the mechanical tomato harvester is an excellent example of the manner in which technology can help some groups while harming others. In the final analysis, however, technology is neutral, although the manner in which it is used may be beneficial or harmful while those who employ it may be arbitrary or magnanimous.

NOTES
1. Wayne D. Rasmussen, "Advances in American Agriculture: The Mechanical Tomato Harvester as a Case Study," *Technology and Culture*, 9 (Oct. 1968): 533.
2. *Ibid.*, 533-534; B. A. Stout and S. K. Ries, "Development of a Mechanical Tomato Harvester," *Agricultural Engineering*, 41 (Oct. 1960): 685.
3. Rasmussen, "Advances in American Agriculture," 532-533.
4. *Ibid.*; John Vandermeer, "Agricultural Research and Social Conflict," *Science for the People*, 11 (Jan./Feb. 1981): 5; Andrew Schmitz and David Seckler, "Mechanized Agriculture and Social Welfare: The Case of the Tomato Harvester," *American Journal of Agricultural Economics*, 52 (Nov. 1970): 570.
5. Raymon E. Webb and W. M. Bruce, "Redesigning the Tomato for Mechanized Production," *Yearbook of Agriculture, 1968*, 103-104; Stout and Ries, "Development of a Mechanical Tomato Harvester," 682-683; Rasmussen, "Advances in American Agriculture," 534.
6. Rasmussen, "Advances in American Agriculture," 535-536.
7. Robert C. Pearl, "1961 Tomato Mechanical Harvest Research in California," *Food Technology*, 16 (July 1962): 54; Rasmussen," Advances in American Agriculture," 536.
8. Rasmussen, "Advances in American Agriculture," 536-537.

9. *Ibid.*, 538.
10. Webb and Bruce, "Redesigning the Tomato for Mechanized Production," 104, 107; Rasmussen, "Advances in American Agriculture," 538-539.
11. Rasmussen, "Advances in American Agriculture," 539-540.
12. *Ibid.*, 541-542.
13. G. H. Sullivan and G. E. Wilcox, "Tomato Mechanization Stalls in Midwest," *American Vegetable Grower*, 22 (Sept. 1974): 14-15.
14. Richard C. Fluck, James W. Strobel, and Herbert H. Bryan, "Field Evaluation of Fruit Detachment of Machine Harvest Tomato Varieties with a Portable Shaker," *Proceedings of the Florida State Horticultural Society*, 81 (1968): 126-127.
15. W. W. Deen, *et al.*, "Recent Advances in Mechanization of Fresh-Market Tomato Harvesting in Florida," *Proceedings of the Florida State Horticultural Society*, 83 (1970): 131-133.
16. *Ibid.*, 133-134; E. T. Sims, Jr., C. E. Hood, and B. K. Webb, "Evaluation of a Totally Mechanized Tomato Harvesting System," *Proceedings of the Florida State Horticultural Society*, 89 (1976): 139; J. S. Lytle, J. S. Barton, and C. E. Hood, "Economic Feasibility of Using the Clemson Tomato Harvester for Fresh-Market Tomatoes," South Carolina Agricultural Experiment Station, *Bulletin 614* (1978), 5-6.
17. Deen, *et al.*, "Recent Advances in Mechanization of Fresh-Market Tomato Harvesting in Florida," 134; Philip L. Martin and Alan L. Olmstead, "The Agricultural Mechanization Controversy," *Science*, 227 (8 Feb. 1985): 602; Chuck Woods, "Tomato Growers Urged to Begin Using New Semi-harvester 'Now'," *Sunshine State Agricultural Research Report*, 17 (Jan./Feb. 1972): 7, 9.
18. "MH-1 Is First Step toward Development of 'Perfect' Tomato for Mechanical Harvest," *Sunshine State Agricultural Research Report*, 17 (Jan./Feb. 1972): 10-11; Chuck Woods, "Tomato Harvester Could 'Neutralize' Mexican Competition," *Citrus and Vegetable Magazine*, 36 (Oct. 1970): 18.
19. Lytle, Barton, and Hood, "Economic Feasibility of Using the Clemson Tomato Harvester," 3; Paul E. Read and D. J. Fieldhouse, "Use of Growth Retardants for Increasing Tomato Yields and Adaptation for Mechanical Harvest," *Journal of the American Horticultural Society*, 95 (Jan. 1970): 73.
20. "Harvesting the Table Tomato," *Agricultural Engineering*, 59 (June 1978): 10-11; H. H. Bryan and W. W. Deen, Jr., "Conditioning Tomatoes for Fresh-Market Machine Harvest," *Proceedings of the Florida State Horticultural Society*, 85 (1972): 156-160.
21. Sims, "Evaluation of a Totally Mechanized Tomato Harvesting System," 139-140; L. N. Shaw, "A Plant Cutter with a Three Apron Pickup for Tomato Harvesters," *Proceedings of the Florida State Horticultural Society*, 92 (1979): 129-130; Norman C. Hayslip and W. W. Deen, "The Modified IFAS Semi-Mechanical Fresh-Market Tomato Harvester," Ft. Pierce ARC Research Report RL 1979-2 (Apr. 1979).
22. J. Francis Cooper, "New Design in Mechanical Tomato Harvester," *Florida Grower & Rancher*, 72 (Aug. 1979): 16; John Hull, "Fresh Tomato Mechanical Harvesting Research Continues," *Citrus and Vegetable Magazine*, 44 (Aug. 1981): 27-28.
23. Schmitz and Seckler, "Mechanized Agriculture and Social Welfare," 569-573.
24. John H. Vandermeer, "Mechanized Agriculture and Social Welfare: The Tomato Harvester in Ohio," *Agriculture and Human Values*, 3 (Summer 1986): 23.
25. Peter M. Rosset and John H. Vandermeer, "The Confrontation Between Processors and Farm Workers in the Midwest Tomato Industry and the Role of the Agricultural Research Extension Establishment," *Agricultural and Human Values*, 3 (Summer 1986): 26; Vandermeer, "Agricultural Research and Social Conflict," 26.
26. Rosset and Vandermeer, "The Confrontation Between Processors and Farm Workers," 26-31.
27. *Ibid.*, 26-28; Vandermeer, "Agricultural Research and Social Conflict," 26; Vandermeer, "Mechanized Agriculture and Social Welfare," 23; Rosset and Vandermeer, "The Confrontation Between Processors and Farm Workers, 29.
28. Rosset and Vandermeer, "The Confrontation Between Processors and Farm Workers," 29-31.
29. Martin and Olmstead, "The Agricultural Mechanization Controversy," 601-602.
30. *Ibid.*
31. *Ibid.*, 605.
32. Rosset and Vandermeer, "The Confrontation Between Processors and Farm Workers," 29-30; Jon A. Brandt and Ben C. French, "Mechanical Harvesting and the California Tomato Industry; A Simulation Analysis," *American Journal of Agricultural Economics*, 65 (May 1983): 265-267.
33. *1974 Census of Agriculture*, I-22; C. S. Kim, *et al.*, "Economic Impacts on Consumers, Growers, and Processors Resulting from Mechanical Tomato Harvesting in California — Revisited," *Journal of Agricultural Economics Research*, 39 (Spring 1987): 39, 42; Martin and Olmstead, "The Agricultural Mechanization Controversy," 602.
34. *1987 Census of Agriculture*, 38; R. W. Hepler, R. F. Fletcher, and T. D. Cordrey, "Varieties and Methods of Planting Determined to Use Tomato Harvester," *Science in Agriculture*, 23 (Fall 1975): 2-3.

Epilogue

TECHNOLOGICAL changes that enabled the invention of tractors, cotton pickers, combines, and sugar and tomato harvesters and the improvement of irrigation were not, of course, the only hardware innovations that affected agriculture in the West. Other important twentieth-century innovations include the development of ensilage cutters that harvest and process the corn crop in one operation for storage. This implement saves time in the field and at the silo, and it enables farmers to raise more livestock as well because farmers can handle more feed in less time than they can with separate cutting and chopping machinery. Mechanical tree shakers with catching frames now enable fruit and nut farmers to harvest almonds, prunes, walnuts, and citrus fruits with less labor than ever before. Heaters, blowers, and sprinklers protect the fruit crops from frost. Furthermore, researchers are working to perfect implements that will harvest cling peaches, asparagus, lettuce, and boysenberries. Moreover, electricity powers a host of implements and provides light and heat for farm homes and work areas. Mechanical milking machines have replaced hand labor in commercial dairying, and mechanized dispensers feed beef cattle and poultry in confined areas. Airplanes "dust" crops with pesticides and herbicides and seed clouds with silver iodide for rain — all of which saves time and labor costs and increases production.[1]

One of the most important agricultural developments since the end of World War II involves the decreased use of technology for seed-bed preparation. This procedure, called no tillage or minimum tillage agriculture, involves planting crops through the stubble without plowing. Then, farmers use herbicides instead of cultivators to control weeds. Minimum tillage agriculture saves fuel, conserves soil and water, and enables farmers to plant lands that would be subject to soil erosion without continuous vegetative cover. Moreover, minimum tillage permits multiple cropping, because a second crop can be planted immediately after the first crop has been harvested, if the growing season is long enough. Smaller tractors are used for minimum tillage agriculture than for conventional plowing. Disks, plows, harrows, and cultivators are no longer needed, but harvesting equipment and special planters are required. Although minimum tillage procedures handled only 2 percent of the agricultural lands in 1975, the United States Department of Agriculture estimated that as much as 45 percent of the nation's agricultural land may be farmed with no tillage methods by the turn of the twenty-first century. The major factors that will determine the future extent of minimum tillage agriculture will be energy costs for the preparation of herbicides and pesticides and the environmental hazards that those chemicals pose for the environment.[2]

Future Trends

Future trends in agricultural technology may enable the cultivation of the ocean floor. Rapid population growth as well as prolonged famine may stimulate technological change that will enable marine farmers to raise photo- and zoo-plankton that have high protein and fat values and vitamins. World food demands may make viable the cultivation of many plants that now are unused or under utilized because of economic reasons. If so, an entirely new level of technological development will be necessary. Technological change also may enable farmers to process crops for consumption before leaving the field. This development would capture the fresh flavor of vegetables and provide the farmer with a higher percentage of the consumer's dollar. Like wine, estate-packaged fruits and vegetables may be achieved, under certain economic conditions, with the proper technological development. The development of a crab-processing machine, for example, would eliminate the need for hand labor, and it would make crab raising profitable. Biotechnology will provide even greater potential change in agricultural production.

In the future, if farmers remain confronted with an uncertain petroleum supply, they may be able to use wind, solar, and tidal power to generate electricity for heating homes and for powering machinery. Nuclear energy also may have potential, if problems of waste disposal, safety, and reduction of scale can be solved. Indeed, just as the Civil War triggered the first agricultural revolution when farmers rapidly switched from hand-powered to horse-powered implements, and just as World War II fostered a second agricultural revolution when farmers increasingly adopted the petrofueled tractor to replace horses, new technological developments in the field of energy production may stimulate a third revolution in American agriculture. Whether that technological change is evolutionary or revolutionary, however, computers will play a major role. Certainly, home computers will not only help keep financial and productivity records, but will also enable the increased automation of many farm tasks.[3]

Retrospective

During the twentieth century, the adoption of new agricultural technology, together with advances in biological and chemical science, made farmers more productive. In 1900, for example, farmers primarily used horse-drawn grain drills and binders to produce about 600 million bushels of wheat that averaged 12 bushels per acre. By

1987 diesel-powered tractors and combines helped wheat farmers produce an estimated 1.8 billion bushels with an average yield of 37.6 bushels per acre. At the turn of the twentieth century, the corn crop averaged 28 bushels per acre and totaled 2.7 billion bushels; in 1987 the crop averaged 119 bushels per acre for a harvest of 6.7 billion bushels. In 1900 cotton farmers, using hand labor for cultivating and harvesting, produced five million pounds with an average of 195 pounds per acre. By 1987, the mechanized cotton crop averaged 706 pounds per acre and totaled seven million pounds. Technological change also made farmers more efficient. At the turn of the twentieth century, 15 man-hours were required per acre of wheat, but only 2.6 man-hours in the mid-1980s. Corn required 38 and 3.1 man-hours per acre, respectively, for those years; and in 1900 cotton required 123 man-hours per acre, but only five man-hours 86 years later. Thus, technological change gave farmers more time for recreational or other work activities.[4]

Increased productivity also meant that each farmer could feed more people than ever before. At the turn of the twentieth century, every farmer provided food and fiber for seven people; by 1986 each farmer provided for 93 people. As productivity increased, fewer farms were required to provide the nation's food supply. As a result, the number of farms declined from 5.7 million in 1900 to 2 million by 1987. Farms also became larger. In 1900 farms averaged 147 acres. Eighty-seven years later, the average farm encompassed 462 acres. Fewer farm workers were needed as well. In 1910, for example, more than 13.5 million people worked on farms; by 1987 2.9 million were so employed. Technology freed farmers from a dependence on costly hired labor and the threat of labor shortages at harvest time. Since farmers cannot pass on the cost of labor, because they do not control the price of their commodities, technology enables them to offset labor costs by achieving greater productivity. Moreover, technology helps reduce the risks inherent in agriculture when timeliness is a critical factor, such as during the harvest season. By the 1980s, a farmer could cultivate from five to eight times as much land as he could a generation before and complete that work faster, more easily, and more efficiently. Moreover, technology enables the majority of the family farmers to operate an economically sound business. Still, the high cost of technology (*e.g.*, two-wheel and four-wheel drive tractors that sell for more than $35,000 and $71,000, respectively; self-propelled combines of medium and large capacity at $54,000 and $76,000; four-row corn heads for a combine at $10,000; and self-propelled, two-row cotton pickers at more than $56,000) discourages young men and women from remaining on the family farm or prevents them from beginning operations of their own. Indeed, the technological investment needed to begin farming easily can exceed $250,000.[5]

Finally, while many innovations in the nineteenth century originated in the machine shops of farmer-mechanics as well as in the research departments of major implement companies, the land-grant universities and the United States Department of Agriculture have contributed engineering expertise and financial support for many of the technological developments in the twentieth century. Furthermore, the land-grant universities, the state agricultural experiment stations, and the United States Department of Agriculture have helped to educate farmers about the benefits of this new technology and have taught them how to use it properly.[6]

Certainly, technological change has had a profound effect on American agriculture and life. It has eased the drudgery of farm tasks, increased productivity, and necessitated an increase in farm size. Technological change also has been an important cause in the decline in farm population. In 1900 nearly 30 million or 41.9 percent of the population lived on farms. Eighty-seven years later, only 2 percent of the population or about 5 million resided on farms. Indeed, technological change, mechanical as well as biological, has relegated the farmer to minority status in American society. Moreover, technological change in agriculture has had a multiplier effect on economic development. Self-propelled implements, for example, have placed increased demands on oil producers and refiners. New machines have helped support iron and steel production and stimulated metallurgical change. Mechanics, salesman, and parts suppliers have appeared to service and sell this new technology. Extended markets, efficient transportation systems, adequate credit institutions, new food processing techniques, and better storage facilities also have been developed to meet the needs of farmers who have increased their productivity with technology.[7]

Technological change, however, has had social costs. As farm population declined, for example, rural schools and churches closed and people who might have lived and worked on farms moved to an urban environment. Certainly, technological change has made farm work easier, but it has displaced many agricultural workers, and it has changed the course of lives and the living patterns of several million people. One cannot always say with certainty that the black sharecropper whom the cotton picker helped replace or the migrant worker whom the sugar beet and tomato harvesters eliminated are leading better lives because the machines removed them from "stoop" labor in the fields, even though the landowners who invested in those machines are profiting from that technology. The Rust brothers, for example, recognized the potentially adverse social and economic consequences of the cotton picker, and they attempted to regulate the sale and use of the machine so that large numbers of people would not be displaced immediately. They failed in those endeavors, and the moral and ethical problems of using technology to replace human labor remains an important issue, particularly in times of high unemployment. Technology, of course, is neither good nor evil. Rather, it is beneficial for some groups and harmful to others at any specific time. Technology, for example, has not been entirely helpful for some agricultural workers, small-scale farmers with limited capital, and individuals who are unaware of the best financial management practices. In general economic and nutritional terms, however, technological change has greatly benefited the quality of farm life and American society.[8]

In retrospect, technological change in agriculture, as in other areas, depends upon three criteria — cumulative knowledge, perceived need, and cost. No one, of course, can foresee what present knowledge will combine with future needs and economic conditions to produce new technological developments for agriculture. Perhaps, technological innovations currently unknown will be commonplace before the end of the twentieth century. Properly developed and applied, however, new forms of agricultural technology will enable farmers to maintain high productivity and to improve the quality of farm life.[9]

NOTES

1. Roy Bainer, "Science and Technology in Western Agriculture," *Agricultural History*, 49 (Jan. 1975): 68-70, 72; Wayne D. Rasmussen, "The Mechanization of Agriculture," *Scientific American*, 247 (Sept. 1982): 86; Clark C. Spence, "Early Uses of Electricity in American Agriculture," *Technology and Culture*, 3 (Spring 1962): 142-160; Eldon W. Downs and George F. Lemmer, "Origins of Aerial Crop Dusting," *Agricultural History*, 39 (July 1965): 123-135; Clark C. Spence, "The Cloud Crackers: Moments in the History of Rainmaking," *Journal of the West*, 18 (Oct. 1979): 63-71.

2. Patricia J. Devlin, "Minimum Tillage — Energy Saving on the Farm," *Journal of NAL Associates*, 4 (Jan./June 1979): 13-16; "Farming Minus the Plow," *Farm Index* (May 1976): 18-20.

3. Wayne D. Rasmussen, "Agriculture in the Future: An Historian's View," *Red River Valley Historical Review*, 3 (Winter 1978): 9-22.

4. *Agricultural Statistics, 1981*: 1, 30, 61; *Agricultural Statistics, 1936*: 5, 33, 75; *Historical Statistics of the United States: Colonial Times to 1970*, pt. 1 (Washington, D.C.: Government Printing Office, 1975), 500; *1987 Census of Agriculture*, 80; *Statistical Abstract of the United States, 1989*, 601, 646, 649.

5. *Historical Statistics of the United States*, 457, 498; *Agricultural Statistics, 1981*, 415, 429; *Agricultural Prices*, 30 Sept. 1980, 45; *Agricultural Prices*, 30 June 1981, 33; Fite, Gilbert C., *American Farmers: The New Minority* (Bloomington: Indiana University Press, 1981), 184, 234; Wayne D. Rasmussen, "The Mechanization of American Agriculture," In *Agricultural Literature: Proud Heritage — Future Promise: A Bicentennial Symposium, September 24-26, 1975*, Alan Fusoni and Leila Moran, eds. (Washington, D.C.: Associates of the National Agricultural Library, Inc., and the Graduate School Press, United States Department of Agriculture, 1977), 312; Phone Interview With Douglas Bowers, History Section, United States Department of Agriculture, 14 May 1990; *1987 Census of Agriculture*, 43, 49; *Statistical Abstract of the United States, 1989*, 626.

6. Rasmussen, "The Mechanization of American Agriculture," 311.

7. *Historical Statistics of the United States*, 457; *Statistical Abstract of the United States, 1989*, 626.

8. James H. Street, *The New Revolution in the Cotton Economy* (Chapel Hill: University of North Carolina Press, 1957): 126-128; Carroll W. Pursell, Jr., "Government and Technology in the Great Depression," *Technology and Culture*, 20 (Jan. 1979): 162-174.

9. R. Douglas Hurt, *American Farm Tools: From Hand-Power to Steam-Power* (Manhattan, KS: Sunflower University Press, 1982), 5-6.

Fort Morgan Public Library
414 Main Street
Fort Morgan, CO

Suggested Readings

Ankli, Robert E., "Horses vs. Tractors on the Corn Belt," *Agricultural History*, 54 (Jan. 1980): 134-148.

Ankli, Robert E. and Alan L. Olmstead, "The Adoption of the Gasoline Tractor in California," *Agricultural History*, 55 (July 1981): 213-230.

Arrington, Leonard J., *Beet Sugar in the West: A History of the Utah-Idaho Sugar Company, 1891-1966* (Seattle: University of Washington Press, 1966).

Bainer, Roy, "Science and Technology in Western Agriculture," *Agricultural History*, 49 (Jan. 1975): 56-72.

Baker, E. J., "A Quarter Century of Tractor Development," *Agricultural Engineering*, 12 (June 1931): 206-207.

Bowen, Leslie, "Irrigated Field Crops on the Great Plains," *Agricultural Engineering*, 19 (Jan. 1938): 13-16.

Brandhorst, L. Carl, "The North Platte Oasis: Notes on the Geography and History of an Irrigated District," *Agricultural History*, 51 (Jan. 1977): 166-177.

_____, "The Panacea of Irrigation: Fact or Fancy," *Journal of the West*, 7 (Oct. 1968): 491-509.

Carroll, Tom, "Basic Requirements in the Design and Development of the Self-Propelled Combine," *Agricultural Engineering*, 29 (Mar. 1948): 101-105.

Daniel, Pete, *Breaking the Land: The Transformation of Cotton, Tobacco, and Rice Cultures Since 1880* (Urbana: University of Illinois Press, 1985).

_____, "The Transformation of the Rural South 1930 to the Present," *Agricultural History*, 55 (July 1981): 231-248.

Downs, Eldon W., and George F. Lemmer, "Origins of Aerial Crop Dusting," *Agricultural History*, 39 (July 1965): 123-135.

Drache, Hiram M., *Beyond the Furrow: Some Keys to Successful Farming in the Twentieth Century* (Danville, IL: Interstate Printers, 1976).

Fite, Gilbert C., *America Farmers: The New Minority* (Bloomington: Indiana University Press, 1981).

_____, *Cotton Fields No More: Southern Agriculture, 1865-1980* (Lexington: University of Kentucky Press, 1984).

_____, "Recent Progress in the Mechanization of Cotton Production in the United States," *Agricultural History*, 24 (Jan. 1950): 19-28.

Fraser, Colin, *Tractor Pioneer: The Life of Harry Ferguson* (Athens: Ohio University Press, 1973).

Gittins, Bert S., *Land of Plenty* (Chicago: Farm Implement Institute, 1959).

Gray, R. B., *The Agricultural Tractor, 1855-1950* (St. Joseph, MI: American Society of Agricultural Engineers, 1975).

Green, Donald E., *Land of the Underground Rain: Irrigation on the Texas High Plains, 1910-1970* (Austin: University of Texas Press, 1973).

Hagan, C. R., "Twenty-Five Years of Cotton Picker Development," *Agricultural Engineering*, 32 (Nov. 1951): 593-596, 599.

Hardy, E. A., "The Combine in the Prairie Provinces," *Agricultural Engineering*, 10 (Feb. 1929): 55-56.

Helms, Douglas, "Technological Methods for Boll Weevil Control," *Agricultural History*, 53 (Jan. 1979): 286-299.

Hightower, Jim, and Susan DeMarco, *Hard Tomatoes, Hard Times: A Report of the Agribusiness Accountability Project on the Failure of America's Land Grant College Complex* (Cambridge, MA: Schenkman Publishing Company, 1973).

Hilliard, Sam B., "The Dynamics of Power: Recent Trends in Mechanization on the American Farm," *Technology and Culture*, 12 (Jan. 1972): 1-24.

Hurlbut, L. W., "More Efficient Corn Harvesting," *Agricultural Engineering*, 36 (Dec. 1955): 791-792.

Hurt, R. Douglas, *American Farm Tools: From Hand-Power to Steam-Power* (Manhattan, KS: Sunflower University Press, 1982).

_____, "Irrigation in the Kansas Plains Since 1930," *Red River Valley Historical Review*, 4 (Summer 1979): 64-72.

_____, "P. P. Haring: Innovator in Cotton Harvesting Technology," *Agricultural History*, 53 (Jan. 1979): 300-307.

_____, "REA: A New Deal for Farmers," *Timeline*, 2 (Dec. 1985/Jan. 1986): 32-47.

_____, "Technological Change in Twentieth-Century Agriculture," in *Technology in the Twentieth Century*, edited by Frank J. Coppa and Richard Harmond (Dubuque, IA: Kendall/Hunt Publishing Co., 1983).

_____, *The Dust Bowl: An Agricultural and Social History* (Chicago: Nelson-Hall, Publishers, 1981).

Isern, Thomas D., *Bull Threshers and Bindlestiffs: Harvesting & Threshing on the North American Plains* (Lawrence: University Press of Kansas, 1990).

_____, *Custom Combining on the Great Plains: A History* (Norman: University of Oklahoma Press, 1981).

Jewkes, John, *The Sources of Invention* (New York: St. Martin's Press, 1959).

Johnson, A. N., "The Impact of Farm Machinery on the Farm Economy," *Agricultural History*, 24 (Jan. 1950): 58-62.

Kirkendall, Richard S., "Up to Now: A History of American Agriculture from Jefferson to Revolution to Crisis," *Agriculture and Human Values*, 4 (Winter 1987): 4-26.

Leviticus, Louis I., "Tractor Testing in the World," *Agricultural History*, 54 (Jan. 1979): 167-172.

Logan, C. A., "The Development of a Corn Combine," *Agricultural Engineering*, 12 (July 1931): 277-278.

Lorenzen, Colby, and G. C. Hanna, "Mechanical Harvesting of Tomatoes," *Agricultural Engineering*, 43 (Jan. 1962): 16-19.

MacGregor, W. F., "The Combined Harvester-Thresher," *Agricultural Engineering*, 6 (May 1925): 100-103.

McCulloch, Alan W., and John F. Schrunk, *Sprinkler Irrigation* (Washington, D.C.: Sheiry Press, 1955).

McKibbin, E. G. "The Development of a Corn Combine," *Agricultural Engineering*, 10 (July 1929): 231-232.

Marcus, Alan I, and Howard P. Segal, *Technology in America: A Brief History* (San Diego: Harcourt Brace Jovanovich, Publishers, 1989).

Martin, Philip L., and Alan L. Olmstead, "The Agricultural Mechanization Controversy," *Science*, 227 (8 Feb. 1985): 601-606.

Musoke, Moses, and Alan L. Oldsters, "The Rise of the Cotton Industry in California: A Comparative Perspective," *Journal of Economic History*, 43 (June 1982): 385-412.

Norbeck, Jack, *Encyclopedia of Steam Traction Engines* (Sarasota, FL: Crestline Publishing Company, 1976).

Peterson, Willis, and Yoav Kislev, "The Cotton Harvester in Retrospect: Labor Displacement or Replacement?" *Journal of Economic History*, 46 (Mar. 1986): 199-216.

Pursell, Carroll W., Jr., "Government and Technology in the Great Depression," *Technology and Culture*, 20 (Jan. 1979): 162-174.

Quick, Graeme, and Wesley Buchele, *The Grain Harvesters* (St. Joseph, MI: American Society of Agricultural Engineers, 1978).

Rasmussen, Wayne D., "Advances in American Agriculture: The Mechanical Tomato Harvester as a Case Study," *Technology and Culture*, 9 (Oct. 1968): 531-543.

———, "Technological Change in Western Sugar Beet Production," *Agricultural History*, 41 (Jan. 1967): 31-36.

———, "The Impact of Technological Change on American Agriculture, 1867-1962," *Journal of Economic History*, 20 (Dec. 1962): 578-591.

———, "The Mechanization of Agriculture," *Scientific American*, 247 (Sept. 1982): 76-89.

Rowan, James E., "Mechanization of the Sugar Beet Industry of Scottsbluff County, Nebraska," *Economic Geography*, 24 (July 1948): 174-180.

Rust, John, "The Origin and Development of the Cotton Picker," *West Tennessee Historical Society Papers*, 7 (1953): 1-21.

Sayre, Charles R., "Cotton Mechanization Since World War II," *Agricultural History*, 53 (Jan. 1979): 105-124.

Schlebecker, John T. "Henry Ford's Tractor," *Smithsonian Journal of History*, 2 (Summer 1967): 63-64.

———, *Whereby We Thrive: A History of American Farming, 1607-1972* (Ames: Iowa State University Press, 1975).

Schmitz, Andrew, and David Seckler, "Mechanized Agriculture and Social Welfare: The Case of the Tomato Harvester," *American Journal of Agricultural Economics*, 52 (Nov. 1970): 659-677.

Sherow, James E., "Utopia, Reality, and Irrigation: The Plight of the Fort Lyon Canal Company in the Arkansas River Valley," *Western Historical Quarterly*, 20 (May 1989): 163-184.

Shover, John L., *First Majority — Last Minority: The Transformation of Rural Life in America* (Dekalb: Northern Illinois University Press, 1976).

Smith, Harris P., "Late Developments in Mechanical Cotton Harvesting," *Agricultural Engineering*, 27 (July 1946): 321-322.

Spence, Clark C., "Early Uses of Electricity in American Agriculture," *Technology and Culture*, 3 (Spring 1962); 142-160.

Splinter, William E., "Center-Pivot Irrigation," *Scientific American*, 234 (June 1976): 90-99.

Stout, B. A., and S. K. Ries, "Development of a Mechanical Tomato Harvester," *Agricultural Engineering*, 41 (Oct. 1960): 682-685.

Street, James H., *The New Revolution in the Cotton Economy* (Chapel Hill: University of North Carolina Press, 1957).

Tucker, Joe, "The Self-Propelled Combine," *Agricultural Engineering*, 25 (Sept. 1944): 333-336, 348.

Wendel, C. H., *Encyclopedia of American Farm Tractors* (Sarasota, FL: Crestline Publishing Co., 1975).

———, *150 Years of International Harvester* (Sarasota, FL: Crestline Publishing Co., 1981).

Whatley, Warren C., "Labor for the Picking: The New Deal in the South," *Journal of Economic History*, 43 (Dec. 1983): 905-929.

———, "Southern Agrarian Labor Contracts as Impediments to Cotton Mechanization," *Journal of Economic History*, 47 (Mar. 1987): 45-70.

Wik, Reynold M., "Henry Ford's Science and Technology for Rural America," *Technology and Culture*, 3 (Summer 1962): 247-258.

———, "Henry Ford's Tractors and American Agriculture," *Agricultural History*, 38 (Apr. 1964): 79-86.

Woodward, Guy O., *Sprinkler Irrigation* (Washington, D.C.: Darby Printing Co., 1959).

Index

by Lori L. Daniel

Other titles of interest from

Sunflower University Press ®

AMERICAN FARM TOOLS: FROM HAND-POWER TO STEAM-POWER, by R. Douglas Hurt

THE DREAD OF PLENTY: AGRICULTURAL RELIEF ACTIVITIES OF THE FEDERAL GOVERNMENT IN THE MIDDLE WEST, 1933-1939, by Michael W. Schuyler

THE RISE OF THE WHEAT STATE: A HISTORY OF KANSAS AGRICULTURE, 1861-1986, edited by George E. Ham and Robin Higham

THE UY RANCH: REMINISCENCES OF A MONTANA STOCK-MAN'S WIFE — 1912-1921, by Helen Addison Howard

HARVESTING SHADOWS: UNTOLD TALES FROM THE FUR TRADE, by H. D. Smiley

DEREVNIA'S DAUGHTERS: SAGA OF AN ALASKAN VILLAGE, by Lola Harvey

FORTUNES FROM THE EARTH: AN HISTORY OF THE BASE AND INDUSTRIAL MINERALS OF SOUTHEAST ALASKA, by Patricia Roppel

Write or call for brochure and backlist.

Sunflower University Press ®

1531 Yuma (Box 1009)
Manhattan, Kansas 66502-4228, USA
Phone 913-539-1888